SPLENDID SERVICE

The Restoration of David Tannenberg's
Home Moravian Church Organ

OLD SALEM INC.
WINSTON-SALEM, NORTH CAROLINA

This book was published to commemorate the restoration and rededication of David Tannenberg's 1800 Home Moravian Church organ. The recitals, symposium, and other special events to celebrate the restored organ were held March 19–21, 2004, in the Old Salem Visitor Center's James A. Gray Jr. Auditorium.

The paper used for this publication meets the minimum American National Standard for Information Sciences—Permanence of Paper for Printed Library Materials, ANSI Z39-48-1984.∞™ and contains 20% post-consumer fiber.

LIBRARY OF CONGRESS CATALOGING-IN-PUBLICATION DATA

Splendid service : the restoration of David Tannenberg's Home Moravian
    Church Organ.
        p. cm
    "This book was published to commemorate the restoration and rededication of
    David Tannenberg's 1800 Home Moravian Church organ. The recitals, symposium,
    and other special events to celebrate the restored organ were held March 19–21, 2004
    in the Old Salem Visitor Center's James A. Gray Jr. Auditorium."
    ISBN 1-879704-08-0 (alk. paper)
    1. Organ (Musical instrument)—North Carolina—Winston-Salem.
2. Organ builders—Pennsylvania.   3. Tannenberg, David.
ML561.S65 2004
786.5'1975667—dc22

                                                    2004002569

For Ann Crews Ring, whose energy, optimism, and commitment made the restoration of the Home Church Tannenberg organ possible, and whose father, Hall Crews, was a "bellows pusher" for the organ.

Contents

Foreword

It is fitting that the restoration of the Tannenberg organ for Home Moravian Church should be celebrated in the spring. With the approach of Easter we arrive at that season of year which resonates most strongly with sentiments dear to the hearts of Moravians. It is the time of rebirth, the time that makes things new. How rare it is that an organ that has been dismembered for nearly a century can be resurrected, restored to its original condition and made to play again as it once did. Now, as its large old bellows are again filled with air and its pipes begin to speak, we can sense in its music the life and spirit of those folk who first heard the organ and sang at its dedication long ago. Its long silent pipes fairly sing to us from that bygone day.

The Home Church Tannenberg organ is significant in the history of organ building for many reasons. Not only does it occupy a special place in the life and work of David Tannenberg, America's first organ builder, but also with his other organs it stands as a rare example of a once prominent but now forgotten style of organ building in his native Saxony. Although the Salem organ was completed in 1800 it is best understood as an eighteenth-century artifact. Tannenberg's career spanned over forty years, beginning in 1758. Throughout his lifetime his instruments remained in essence true to the style of organs he had known in his youth in Germany. Over the course of his life his work shows no signs of diminishing standards of quality, which one might expect considering his isolation from other builders in the new world. On the contrary, one can see in his later instruments the refined skills of a man still intensely committed to the best in his craft. More than once the Salem instrument has surprised its restorers with its high degree of technical and artistic sophistication. An organ of lesser quality could hardly have survived the many drastic changes it suffered at the hands of itinerant builders during its first hundred years.

In some ways Tannenberg was ahead of his time. From the outset of his career, in contrast to his European counterparts, he tuned his instruments in equal temperament, a practice that did not gain general acceptance until the middle of the nineteenth century. Likewise, Tannenberg was the first builder known to us who consistently used a system of logarithms to determine the size of his pipes.

The Home Church organ is unique in that it is Tannenberg's only surviving instrument with two manuals and pedal. Its design was unusual for him by his placement of four gentle or "lieblich" stops on the second manual. Several of these stops represent the earliest examples of such sounds in an American instrument. They are particularly suited to the Moravian musical tradition in which other instruments were customarily used with the organ.

It is testimony to the vision of Salem's early settlers that they would have thought so highly of their new church that they would spare nothing to fit it with the finest organ they could obtain. We find it difficult today from our perspective of boundless material wealth and constant exposure to music to appreciate what the arrival of such an instrument must have meant to this frontier community in 1800. There is a telling report that on first hearing a small organ in Bethabara the Indians in Wachovia were convinced that there were not pipes but children inside who were singing. Perhaps if we listen carefully we too can hear in the intimate sounds of the restored organ voices from that quieter and more spiritual time, voices from which we may learn something of value for the nourishment of our world-weary hearts and souls. In this hope we present our handiwork of the past year to the Salem community, with gratitude for the trust you have placed in us for the restoration of this precious instrument.

GEORGE TAYLOR AND JOHN BOODY
Taylor & Boody Organbuilders
Staunton, Virginia

Introduction

Because of its almost unique historical significance as a musical instrument and its testament to the importance of music in Moravian culture, the restoration of the organ made for Home Moravian Church by the Pennsylvania organ builder, David Tannenberg, is a landmark achievement for Old Salem.

Tannenberg's career is representative of the nationally significant Moravian craft tradition that developed in North Carolina and Pennsylvania in the eighteenth century. Organs, with their complex configuration of pipes, stops, wind systems, and windchests, were the high-tech mechanisms of the time. The Home Church organ is perhaps the most significant surviving Tannenberg organ. Tannenberg is credited with building approximately forty organs during a career that began in 1758 and ended in 1804. Unfortunately, only nine organs survive, and many of these have been significantly modified from their original design. The organ built for Home Church, the largest extant example of Tannenberg's work, is the only surviving two-manual Tannenberg organ, and is largely intact. Even more significantly, the organ Tannenberg built for Home Church was the second one he delivered to Salem. The first, a much smaller one-manual organ, was installed in the Salem Gemein Haus in 1798 and can be found today in the Saal of the Single Brothers' House in Salem where it is still heard by visitors everyday.

Tannenberg's Home Church organ remained in the church until 1910 when it was replaced with a larger, modern organ. Many of Tannenberg's organs suffered a similar fate. Some of these were even cut up and distributed as souvenirs to the members of the congrega-tion. As an example of the respect for heritage that has made the preservation and restoration of so much of Salem possible, rather than converting it into souvenirs, the members of Home Moravian Church decided instead to place the organ in storage. It remained in storage at Home Church for over fifty years, until it was turned over to Old Salem for safekeeping in the 1960s along with an assortment of other early Salem artifacts.

It might have remained in storage today, an incongruous mass of pipes and parts, had it not been for the trained eye of then Old Salem Curator, Paula Locklair. While Paula realized the potential significance of the organ, she called on the renowned organ scholar Barbara Owen to inspect both the Home Church organ and the other Tannenberg in use in the Single Brothers' House. Owen concluded that both organs were enormously significant musical instruments. She also concluded that "despite its thoroughly battered appearance, the Home Church organ is remarkably intact and eminently restorable." With this recommendation began a remarkable odyssey that has brought this magnificent instrument back to life.

The first step was to obtain official permission from Home Church to undertake the restoration. This permission was granted by the officials and boards of the church and conveyed to Old Salem by letter from then Pastor Dr. Robert Sawyer on June 14, 1989. An official loan agreement was completed in February 1992. In 1998, the organ was re-assembled for the first time since its removal from Home Church as an exhibit in Old Salem's new Horton Center Gallery. The organ was re-assembled by Taylor & Boody, the renowned organ builders from Staunton, Virginia, who confirmed Barbara Owen's conclusion about the possibilities of restoration. Before the restoration could proceed, however, Old Salem had to find an appropriate home for the restored instrument.

This final challenge fell into place quickly as the new Old Salem Visitor Center was in the final planning stages. It was decided a new auditorium, designed specifically for the organ, would be included in the new center. Consequently, upon the termination of the organ re-assembly exhibit in early 1999, the organ was shipped off to Taylor & Boody's shop in Staunton for restoration. A final, but signifcant part of the organ was also obtained by Old Salem: In addition to retaining the organ, Home Church also retained the original bellows and wind system. Left in place in the Home Church attic when the organ was put into storage, they too were loaned to Old Salem and removed from the church in 2002.

In early 2004, fifteen years since its restoration was initiated, ninety-four years since its removal from Home Church, and 204 years since its original installation, David Tannenberg's organ will arrive back in Salem. The new James A. Gray Jr. Auditorium in the Old Salem Visitor Center has been planned with careful attention to the acoustics of the organ's original home. The original interior of Home Church had a bare floor where the sound had the opportunity to bounce off the hard surfaces. With the assistance of an acoustical engineer, the auditorium has been carefully planned to mimic the original conditions of the Home Church sanctuary.

The restored Tannenberg organ will be a treasure not only for Old Salem, but also for North Carolina and our nation. The organ is a testament to the hard work, creativity, and inspiration of the early European settlers and the enduring role of music in lifting our spirits and celebrating our faith.

PAUL C. REBER, PHD
President, Old Salem Inc.
Winston-Salem, North Carolina

Acknowledgments

The completion of the restoration of David Tannenberg's largest surviving pipe organ has been a fifteen-year project for Old Salem and a nearly one-hundred-year odyssey if one considers the first step of the restoration to be the careful storage of the organ when it was removed from Home Moravian Church in 1910. Any project that spans nearly a century cannot be completed alone, and Old Salem acknowledges a debt of gratitude to many people and organizations that have helped with this project along the way.

Old Salem is profoundly grateful to everyone on the staff of Taylor & Boody Organbuilders for their enthusiasm and scholarship and for the meticulous care they took in studying, documenting, and restoring this organ to its original splendor. All of their names and contributions to this project can be found as an appendix to Bruce Shull's essay about the restoration of the organ.

We are especially grateful to the following organizations and individuals who have so generously contributed financially to the success of this project: Dr. and Mrs. Malcolm Brown; Mr. Charles Babcock Jr.; Dr. Robert H. Harris; A. J. Fletcher Foundation; Home Moravian Church, Home Moravian Women's Fellowship, Home Moravian Men of the Church; Wachovia Historical Society; Mary Duke Biddle Foundation.

Our sincere thanks and appreciation go to authors William Armstrong and Bruce Shull for providing enlightening essays for this book, which document the sojourn of David Tannenberg and this organ so very well, and also to George Taylor, John Boody, and Paul Reber, President of Old Salem, for their meaningful contributions. In addition, we must extend our sincere thanks to Gary Albert, Old Salem's Director of Publications, for his superb job of editing the manuscripts and seeing the book through to publication; to Jennifer Bower, Manager of Photographic Resources, for her diligent work in assembling the photographs; and to Old Salem's Photographer, Wes Stewart.

The Tannenberg Dedication Planning Committee worked diligently to plan and organize the gala events for the weekend of March 19–21, 2004, and we thank them all: Lynda Alexander, Mary Armitage, Scott Carpenter, Stewart Carter, Paula Chamblee, Marcia Deem, Sally Gant, Rickey D. Johnson, Nola Reed Knouse, Laurence Libin, John Mitchener, John and Margaret Mueller, Barbara Owen, Norma Pearman, Kelli Reich, Jean Thomas, and Philip Waggoner.

During the November 1998 Tannenberg Symposium, it was hoped that in the not too distant future there would be another symposium to celebrate the completion of the organ's restoration. Now six years later that milestone has been achieved, and we want to thank the 2004 symposium speakers for their enlightening contributions: Raymond J. Brunner, C. Daniel Crews, Nola Reed Knouse, Laurence Libin, Barbara Owen, Kristian Wegscheider, and Taylor & Boody Organbuilders.

In 1998 it was not possible that music from this organ could be part of the symposium, but the highlight of this March 2004 weekend—and the most widely anticipated event—will be the first public hearing of the organ since 1910. This inaugural concert will be presented by widely lauded organist Peter Sykes, who took great care in selecting his program in a way that would best demonstrate the musical qualities of the organ. Even though the organ is a historic instrument, it is much more than a "museum piece." Originally, from its pipes came the music of its own time as well as the past, and beginning in 2004 the music will again bridge the past and the present.

Both Old Salem and myself personally wish to express our deep gratitude and appreciation to my brother and sister-in-law, Mark and Rosanne Welshimer, for commissioning my wonderful and talented husband, Dan Locklair, to write a new piece for this momentous occasion. Called *Salem Sonata*, this piece will be premiered by

Peter Sykes at the dedicatory recital. We are truly thrilled that new music from our time will help to launch this organ into its second life.

We are also very grateful to Tom Kenan and the William R. Kenan Charitable Trust for establishing a very generous programming endowment, named in honor of Archie and Mary Louise Davis. This endowment will ensure the regular use of the organ for public programs. We also thank the Randleigh Foundation Trust, Mr. and Mrs. Mark J. Welshimer, Mr. Robert E. Grant, and Dr. and Mrs. Dan Locklair for their financial contributions toward public programs for the organ. Our thanks also go to the Home Moravian Church choir and clergy for the liturgical service to rededicate the organ on March 21st, David Tannenberg's 276th birthday.

Old Salem is indebted to past and present staff members who have helped and supported this endeavor for many years, especially John Larson, Johanna Brown, and Norma Pearman.

In addition we offer our sincere thanks to the staff members of the Moravian Music Foundation, and the Moravian Archives in Winston-Salem, Bethlehem, Pennsylvania, and Herrnhut, Germany, who have provided invaluable research assistance. We also greatly appreciate the Home Moravian Church staff, past and present, who not only preserved the organ but also encouraged its restoration.

We are particularly grateful to Barbara Owen, organ historian and consultant, and Ann Ring, Old Salem Trustee and friend: To Barbara for her wise guidance, optimism, and unfailing encouragement in the worthiness of this enormous project; and to Ann for her support, personal interest, commitment, and tireless efforts to successfully raise the necessary funds.

In addition to those already mentioned, Old Salem thanks the following for their financial contributions to this project: Mrs. Lola Culler; Mrs. Helen A. Passano; Mr. and Mrs. William S. Powell; AVAYA; Mr. and Mrs. William R. Lowder; Mr. and Mrs. Raymond C. Ferguson; American Guild of Organists (Winston-Salem Chapter); Mr. Christopher Leonard; Ms. Elizabeth B. Marbury; Mr. and

Mrs. Charles G. McDaniel; Mr. and Mrs. Douglas Quarles; Mrs. Ralph Welshimer; Mr. and Mrs. Clay V. Ring Jr.; Judge and Mrs. J. M. H. Willis Jr.; and Jane Dart Maunsell.

To conclude on a personal note, I extend a very warm and special "thank you" to my husband, Dan, and my mother, Eileen Welshimer, who have shared my enthusiasm and have been so wonderfully interested in every phase of this endeavor.

PAULA LOCKLAIR
Vice President, MESDA
and the Horton Center Museums
Old Salem Inc.
Winston-Salem, North Carolina

David Tannenberg

An Organ Builder's Life

WILLIAM H. ARMSTRONG

D AVID TANNENBERG, the organ builder, was a German-speaking immigrant who lived most of his life in the small Moravian town of Lititz in Pennsylvania. He had no formal training in organ building; instead he learned his profession by working with an experienced organ builder, Johann Gottlob Klemm, also a German-speaking immigrant. Tannenberg learned his profession well, building or helping to build nearly fifty organs in six states and with such excellence that his surviving organs are highly prized today—as the careful renovation of the organ built in 1800 for the Moravian Church in Salem attests.

⁊

Tannenberg's father, Johann Tanneberger, and his mother, Judith Nitschmann Tanneberger, were both from Moravia and were members of the *Unitas Fratrum* (Unity of the Brethren), commonly referred to as the Moravian Church. (The family was known among Moravians as Tanneberger; the organ builder, however, adopted the form Tannenberg and used it rather consistently, despite the fact that others still often referred to him as Tanneberger.)

The members of the Unitas Fratrum were the followers of John Hus, who was burned at the stake in 1415 at Constance, Baden, Germany, for supposed heresies. The society was all but obliterated in the Counter-Reformation but experienced a rebirth in 1722, when some of the strongest families fled from persecution in Moravia to Saxony and found refuge on the estates of Count Nicolaus Ludwig von Zinzendorf.

Johann Tanneberger's family had been among those involved in the rebirth of the Moravian Church, and Johann was among those persecuted for their beliefs. After being arrested twice, Johann, his wife, and a small son fled to Herrnhut, a town on Count Zinzendorf's estates. They later moved to the nearby village of Berthelsdorf, where David Tannenberg was born on March 21, 1728. In 1746, Johann and Judith Tanneberger and their children moved back to Herrnhut, where Johann and Judith lived until their deaths.

From an early age, David Tannenberg was deeply devoted to the Moravians' beliefs. His schoolmaster at Berthelsdorf fostered that devotion, but so did Count Zinzendorf himself. The count arranged for Tannenberg to enter school at the age of ten. Tannenberg studied for four years at various schools in the Wetterau, in Hesse, north of Frankfurt am Main. While he was there, a "Pilgrim Congregation" including Tannenberg accompanied Zinzendorf on a trip to the Swiss cities of Geneva and Basel. Then, when he was fourteen, Tannenberg left school and returned home and later went with his family to Herrnhut and was received into the Moravian congregation there. He remained a faithful member of the Moravian Church all his life, often expressing his gratitude to the one he called Savior for the assistance and blessings he had experienced in his life and work.

In 1748, Tannenberg was called to become part of the Moravian community at Zeist, Holland, but once there he soon joined a group of Moravians who were leaving for a new settlement in Bethlehem, Pennsylvania. On February 20, 1749, the group began a twelve-week journey to America, sailing on the Moravian ship *Irene*.

Tannenberg arrived in Bethlehem on May 21, and on July 15 he was married in what came to be known as "the Great Wedding." He and Anna Rosina Kern, who had traveled to Bethlehem in the same group as Tannenberg, were married with twenty-seven other couples in unions that, in the Moravian fashion, were arranged by the elders of the congregation and then submitted by lot for the Savior to approve or disapprove. The circumstances of the marriage may have seemed unusual to outsiders, but the marriage lasted for nearly forty-three years, until Rosina's death in 1792.

Tannenberg came to Bethlehem as a joiner and in that capacity helped erect buildings for the growing town. In 1752 he and his wife moved to nearby Nazareth, where he became warden, or business manager, of the community. But with the threat of Indian attacks there, the couple moved back to Bethlehem in 1754. In these two communities four of their children were born: Anna Rosina, Maria Elisabeth, Anna Maria, and Johann David.

Tannenberg's career changed with the arrival in Bethlehem of an older Moravian, Johann Gottlob Klemm. Klemm was an organ builder, and he took Tannenberg as his assistant in the repair of an organ and the building of a new organ at Bethlehem and the building of two new organs at Nazareth.

Klemm had learned organ building in Dresden. There he had also become acquainted with Count Zinzendorf and traveled with him to Herrnhut, where Klemm became one of the spiritual leaders of the Moravian Church. But he had a falling out with Zinzendorf and left for Pennsylvania with a group of Schwenkfelders, followers of the spiritualist reformer Caspar Schwenkfeld von Ossig. After his arrival, he built organs for various churches, including Gloria Dei Lutheran Church in Philadelphia, Trinity Episcopal Church in New York City, and the Moravian Chapel in Bethlehem. Renewing his association with the Moravians, the sixty-seven-year-old Klemm moved to Bethlehem in 1757. Soon he had Tannenberg working with him, and he and the Tannenberg family moved to Nazareth where, in addition to the organs for that community and for Bethlehem, they built an organ for the Moravian congregation at nearby Christian's Spring. Moving again, to the Burnside House near Bethlehem, they built another organ, for the Moravian congregation in Bethabara, North Carolina.

Klemm's death in 1762 left Tannenberg's profession in question. The elders tried to discourage him from organ building, perhaps fearing that it would lead to too much contact with the outside world. But Tannenberg chose to continue building organs and apparently convinced the reluctant elders to permit it. His skills as a joiner and the skills he had learned from Klemm were his only training, but they were augmented by the acquisition of a manuscript entitled "The Secretly Kept Art of the Scaling of Organ Pipes," a theoretical work by Georg Andreas Sorge, the Court and City Organist at Lobenstein, Germany, that gave Tannenberg the mathematical basis for the construction of organ pipes.

In 1765, the Tannenberg family moved to the Moravian community of Lititz, in Lancaster County, Pennsylvania. With the birth of another son, Samuel, the following year, there were five children in the family. The Tannenbergs lived in what was known as the *Pilgerhaus,* a two-story stone house that had been the first private house built in Lititz.

Lititz was a community comprised entirely of Moravians and governed by Moravian officials. Private residences like Tannenberg's were permitted, but there were also communal residences known as the Single Sisters' House and the Single Brothers' House where the unmarried residents lived as congregations or "choirs" under the direction of a chaplain and a warden. The rest of the community was also organized into choirs: the married couples, the widows, the widowers, the little boys, little girls, and infants, each with its own worship services, liturgies, hymns, rules, and anniversaries.

The town was governed by strict rules: residents could change their trades or travel outside the community only with the approval of the leaders of the church and could not give a night's lodging to

anyone without approval. The Town Regulations stated that "No Dancing Matches, Taverning (except for the necessary Entertainment of Strangers and Travellers), Beer-Tap[p]ings, Feastings at Weddings, Christenings or Burials, Common Sports & Pastimes, nor the playing of the Children in the Streets, shall be so much as

FIGURE 1. View of the Tannenbergs's home, the *Pilgerhaus* (center), in Lititz, Pennsylvania, 1757, by Nicholas Garrison, Jr. (1726–1802). *Courtesy of the Moravian Archives, Bethlehem, Pennsylvania.*

heard of amongst the Inhabitants. They that have Inclinations that Way bent cannot live at Lititz."[1]

Tannenberg often found himself hedged in by the town's regulations. He was told that he could not raise fruit because it might interfere with his organ building. He was denounced for asking his tailor to make him a pair of red trousers, an act that might lead others to "clothing foolishness."[2] And he was reprimanded for taking his daughter Rosina to a funeral in the country and for helping his son Samuel buy a pocket watch. Yet he remained a loyal resident of the town for thirty-nine years, its benefits far outweighing its restrictions.

Foremost among those benefits was the musical life of the community. Lititz had an orchestra, the *collegium musicum,* and Tannenberg participated in it as a violinist (or perhaps a violist). The orchestra performed for visitors, as when the Attorney General of the United States, Edmund Randolph, visited Lititz in 1791. The library of the orchestra contained chamber works of some fifty European composers, including Boccherini, Handel, Haydn, and Mozart. Tannenberg also contributed to the musical life of Lititz as a vocalist; he and Andreas Albrecht, the village gunsmith, served as the church's *cantores* at the church's festive occasions.

Respected by the community for his business experience and good judgment, Tannenberg served in many administrative offices in Lititz. He was collector or treasurer for various funds and served a term as township assessor, as well as serving on the Church Council and other Moravian committees and conferences.

During the early years in Lititz, Tannenberg built his organs in a large room in his home, but later the work was done in a small, stone shop erected at the rear of his house. An average of one organ a year was built there, almost all—if not all—for German-speaking congregations. Many of the organs were for Moravians, but he also built organs for German Lutheran and Reformed churches and one organ for a Catholic church, St. Mary's Church in Lancaster, Pennsylvania, most of whose members were German. In some cases, the organs were for "union churches," buildings shared by both Lutheran and Reformed congregations. And he built organs for individuals such as "Mr. Fischer" in York, Pennsylvania, and "a man in Philadelphia." The list of organs for churches in Pennsylvania is long, but he also built organs for churches in New York, Maryland, New Jersey, North Carolina, and Virginia. The installation of his organs and the repair and tuning of them and of other organs meant that Tannenberg traveled extensively, often spending weeks or months away from Lititz.

Tannenberg's organs soon won him the admiration of music lovers near and far. A Philadelphia newspaper gave prominent notice to the fifteen-stop organ built for the German Reformed Church in Lancaster, Pennsylvania, in 1770:

The organ was made by David Tanneberger of Lititz—a Moravian town nearby—and I dare venture to assert, is much superior in workmanship and sweetness of sound to any made by the late celebrated Mr. Feyering [Philip Feyring, a German Lutheran organ builder in Philadelphia], who was so generally taken notice of for his ingenuity. It does great honor to the maker and is worth the attention and notice of the curious who may happen to pass this way.[3]

Even greater praise was given to the twenty-stop organ built for Trinity Lutheran Church in Lancaster in 1774. A captured British army officer said later, with some exaggeration, that:

. . . the organ is reckoned the largest and best in America, it was built by a German, who resides about 17 miles from Lancaster, he made every individual part of it with his own hands; it was near 7 years in compleating; the organ has not only every pipe and stop that is in most others, but it has many other pipes to swell the bass, which are of an amazing circumference, and these are played upon by the feet, there being a row of wooden keys that the performer treads on. . . . You wonder it did not take up the man's whole life in constructing.[4]

The revolution against England profoundly affected the Moravians in Lititz and nearly halted Tannenberg's organ building. The

Moravians were opposed to war and tried to avoid any participation in military activities. Church members were counseled to remain loyal to the oath they had taken to the king. They were, however, willing to pay war taxes, and Tannenberg was appointed collector of taxes for Lititz, whose officials considered the taxes "purely a township affair."[5]

The demands on them were increased when all men ages eighteen to fifty-three, including Moravians, were called to be enrolled in the militia. The men of Lititz responded by boycotting the muster, but on October 21, 1777, six armed militiamen entered the chapel of the Single Brothers' House in Lititz and arrested nine men. Five married men were also arrested; among them was forty-nine-year-old David Tannenberg. A diarist in Lititz recorded the events that followed.

The next day they were taken to Lancaster and, to the accompaniment of drum and fife, through a dense mass of people, with cries of "Tories" from every side, were marched to the Quaker meeting house, where they were locked up with many others who, like themselves, had been thus forcibly dragged together. Here their room was so limited that they could neither sit nor lie down; and besides, they had very little to eat.[6]

With the help of influential friends, the men were soon released, but the war continued to intrude on their lives. It was soon announced that General George Washington had chosen Lititz, with its large stone buildings, as the site for a military hospital. On December 19, 1777, eighty sick soldiers arrived and the next day fifteen wagons filled with more soldiers appeared. Still more soldiers arrived, and by January 1, 1778, seven of the soldiers had died.

Dr. William Brown, Physician General of the Middle Department of the Continental Army, was sent to Lititz and placed in charge of all the surrounding hospitals. Dr. Brown was quartered in the Tannenbergs' home and remained there for seven months. The sick and wounded soldiers were in Lititz for nine months—altogether between five hundred and one thousand of them—and one hundred twenty of them died and were buried there.

In 1778, the congregation was divided when twenty-two members went to Lancaster to take an oath of allegiance that the Pennsylvania General Assembly had required and the church officials opposed. Among them were David Tannenberg and seventeen-year-old David Tannenberg Jr. David Jr. strayed even further from the church's wishes in allowing himself to be elected a lieutenant in the Lancaster County Militia. His commission in the militia and his attendance at an unauthorized party outside the village caused the Lititz elders to dismiss him from the community. The elders placed some of the blame for the son's actions on his father, who they said allowed him to "run on the farms and after the girls"[7] and did not punish him or allow him to be punished.

The building of organs was slowed during the war, but after the war they were again in demand. Among the organs Tannenberg built was one for a new Moravian church building in Lititz, for which he also designed the steeple and pulpit. But his greatest success was the organ he built for Zion Lutheran Church in Philadelphia in 1790. It was his largest organ, twenty-four feet wide and twenty-seven feet high, with thirty-four stops and nearly two thousand speaking pipes, more than a hundred of them brightly polished metal pipes visible in the front of the organ. President and Mrs. Washington and members of the Congress and the Pennsylvania Assembly were among those who came to hear the organ played. A reporter who heard it could hardly restrain his enthusiasm:

This great and beautiful creation is the work of Mr. David Tanneberg, of Lititz in Lancaster County, who began to build organs here in America by his own instincts, but through reading, reflection and unwearied industry has raised himself to such a height that if the most skilled European builder should come here and examine this work, in the judgment of experts, he could only bestow praise and be won to him.[8]

Unfortunately, the organ was destroyed in a fire just four years after its installation.

Anna Rosina Tannenberg, the organ builder's wife, died in 1792. With a new awareness of his own mortality, Tannenberg began to search for a partner and possible successor to his business. Both his sons had trained as organ builders, but David Jr. had been dismissed from the community and Samuel had died when he was only twenty-two. (At one time, Tannenberg had considered training one of his daughters as an organ builder, but the Lititz officials, unable to imagine such a thing, would not permit it.) With official permission, Tannenberg wrote to Herrnhut to ask that Philip Bachmann, a Moravian trained in the manufacture of musical instruments, be sent to Lititz to work with him. Bachmann arrived in 1793 and not only began to work with Tannenberg but also married Tannenberg's youngest daughter, Anna Maria.

With Bachmann's assistance, Tannenberg built organs for nine churches in Pennsylvania, a church in Baltimore, Maryland, and two organs for the Moravians in Salem, North Carolina. By the time the organs for North Carolina were built, Tannenberg was no longer able to travel, and Bachmann made the trips and installed the organs. Bachmann spent a year in Salem working on the 1800 organ, and during that time disputes over money caused a rift between the two men. Anna Maria Bachmann had earlier drowned herself in a stream, and without that tie between her husband and her father the rift between the men became permanent. Bachmann did travel to Virginia to install a Tannenberg organ there, and Tannenberg made the metal pipes for one of Bachmann's organs, but Bachmann was soon working independently in Lititz as an instrument maker.

With the help of another assistant, Johannes Schnell, Tannenberg built organs for New Holland, Pennsylvania, and Madison, Virginia, and signed a contract for a nineteen-stop organ for the Moravians in Bethlehem, which he did not live to complete. He suffered a stroke in September 1803 but was well enough the next spring to set out for Christ Lutheran Church in York, Pennsylvania, to install what was to be his last organ. While standing on a bench or scaffold to tune the organ, he apparently suffered another stroke and fell to the floor of the gallery, striking his head. By the time his second wife, Anna Maria Lang, whom he had married in 1800, arrived on May 19, she was informed that her husband had died that morning.

FIGURE 2. Watercolor of David Tannenberg (at left) installing his Christ Lutheran Church organ in York, Pennsylvania. Lewis Miller, c. 1830. Written text at bottom of the drawing reads: "David Danneberger, Organ builder and his Journeyman in the old Lutheran Church, 1807. he was from Litiz, and died in York. at the time working at the organ." *Courtesy of the York County Heritage Trust, Pennsylvania.*

The funeral was held in York on May 21 with the body placed before the altar of the Lutheran Church and Tannenberg's organ playing for the first time. He was buried in the Moravian God's Acre in York as the children of the Moravian and Lutheran churches sang hymns beside his grave.

❧

Other organ builders advertised their services, but there is no record of Tannenberg having done so. Moravians in other communities were well aware of his work, and once he had built a few organs for other religious groups, newspaper reports about them and the exchange of pastors among churches quickly spread his fame.

When a church decided to purchase an organ, the usual practice was to take up a subscription toward the cost. Then, on the basis of the amount pledged, the church would negotiate the cost and the type of organ Tannenberg could provide, a matter Tannenberg approached with both artistic and practical considerations: the other instruments that might be used with the organ, the size of the building, and the space available for the organ. A contract was then signed, which specified the stops to be included in the organ and the timing of the payments. In some cases, the church appointed a committee to superintend the work.

The organs varied greatly in size. The little organ built for the Moravians in Graceham, Maryland, which is now at Lititz, had only four stops. His largest organ, for Zion Lutheran Church in Philadelphia, had thirty-four stops. The smaller organs were built entirely in Lititz. Most of the parts for the larger organs were made in Lititz, but the final assembly and the construction of the cases were done at the site of the installation.

In addition to his sons, his son-in-law Philip Bachmann, and Johannes Schnell, Tannenberg used several other assistants over the years. He could also rely on the skills of the other residents of Lititz: leatherworkers, cabinetmakers, carpenters, blacksmiths, and toolmakers. But the conception of the organs was Tannenberg's, and the making of metal pipes was something he alone felt capable of doing. His contemporaries recognized his skills by calling him "that excellent and ingenious artist" and "a great mechanical genius."[9]

When the smaller organs were finished, they were set up and demonstrated, sometimes drawing crowds of admiring listeners from as far away as Philadelphia. Then the organs, large or small, were packed in wagons to be taken to the sites of their installation.

The churches provided the teams and wagons (the familiar blue-and-red, canvas-covered Conestoga wagons), and Tannenberg took great care to arrange the delicate parts in the wagons and protect them with straw so they would not be damaged.

The installation of the smaller organs took only a few days, but weeks or even months might be required for the larger ones. Tannenberg and his assistants spent at least three-and-a-half months installing the organ in Zion Lutheran Church in Philadelphia, with room and board provided by the congregation.

The organs were usually placed in the gallery of the church, most often in the rear but occasionally in one of the side galleries. That was also true in the Moravian churches, but the Moravian chapels were simply rooms in the congregation houses, and there the organs stood among the worshipers, as the 1798 organ does today in the *Saal*, or chapel, of the Single Brothers' House in Old Salem, North Carolina. Wherever they were placed, the organs were things of beauty. The graceful organ cases were usually painted white with gold pipe shades setting off the lustrous metal of the exposed pipes.

The building and installation of church organs was followed by a public consecration, a worship service usually attended by crowds of church members and visitors and long remembered in the communities. When the organ for the Moravian congregation near Lebanon, Pennsylvania, was consecrated, so many people came from the town and the countryside that extra benches had to be provided—and still the chapel could not contain the crowd. In that service, violinists from the congregation accompanied the playing of the organ. Trombonists from Lititz went to nearby Lancaster for the consecration of Tannenberg's new organ in the Lancaster Moravian Church. On Saturday night they played for the townsfolk from the steeple of the Lutheran Church and on Sunday from the steeple of the Reformed Church. When Tannenberg's organ for the Moravians in Graceham, Maryland, was consecrated in a communion service, the builder himself participated by singing from the church's gallery.

The interest in the organs lasted long beyond their consecration.

Few churches in those days had organs, and one that did was often known simply as "the Organ Church." Tannenberg's organs had many admiring visitors, but perhaps none so unusual as those who attended a council in 1777 at the union church in Easton, Pennsylvania, between several Indian chiefs representing the Six Nations and their confederates and representatives of the Continental Congress, the Pennsylvania Assembly, and the Council of Safety of Pennsylvania. The secretary of the American commissioners, Thomas Paine, the author of *Common Sense,* reported that "the ceremony of shaking hands being gone through, a glass of rum was served round to all the Indians present, and the health of the congress and the Six Nations with the allies were drank. The organ being ordered to play in the mean time."[10]

A few pipes are all that remains of the Easton organ, and most of Tannenberg's other organs are entirely gone. Some, like the large organ in Zion Lutheran Church in Philadelphia, were burned in church fires. Some simply wore out and were replaced, while others were sold to other churches and played in them until they had outlived their usefulness. Nine of the organs survive, most of which have been restored in recent years. Four additional organ cases remain, and in one of them three of the original Tannenberg ranks of pipes were retained.

Only a partial list of the organs Tannenberg built has survived. The following list has been compiled from several sources, including materials in the Archives of the Moravian Church in Bethlehem, Pennsylvania. The dates in most cases are the dates of the organs' installation or consecration. The surviving organs or organ cases are noted by italic type.

THE KLEMM-TANNENBERG ORGANS

1758   Nazareth, Pennsylvania. For the chapel of the Moravian congregation in Nazareth Hall.
1758   Nazareth, Pennsylvania. A smaller organ for another room in Nazareth Hall.

1759　Bethlehem, Pennsylvania. For the chapel of the Moravian congregation.

1760　Christian's Spring, Pennsylvania. For the chapel of the Moravian congregation.

1762　Bethabara, Forsyth County, North Carolina. For the chapel of the Moravian congregation. This small organ is presumed to be the work of Klemm and Tannenberg.

1765　Lancaster, Pennsylvania. For the chapel of the Moravian congregation.

1765 or 1768　York, Pennsylvania. For the chapel of the Moravian congregation.

1766　Philadelphia, Pennsylvania. For "a man in Philadelphia."

1767　Albany, New York. Perhaps for the German Reformed Church.

1768　Maxatawny, Pennsylvania. For the Lutheran Church (now St. John's Church, Kutztown, Berks County).

1769　New Goshenhoppen, Pennsylvania, (near East Greenville, Upper Hanover Township, Montgomery County). For the German Reformed Church.

1770　*Moselem, Pennsylvania. For Zion (Moselem) Lutheran Church, Richmond Township, Berks County.*

1770　Frederick, Maryland. For the German Reformed Church. Tannenberg repaired and set up the organ, but may not have been its builder.

1770　*Lancaster, Pennsylvania. For the German Reformed Church (now First Reformed Church United Church of Christ). The organ was replaced in 1885, but the case—slightly enlarged—is still in the church.*

1771　Reading, Pennsylvania. For Trinity Lutheran Church.

1772　The diary of the Lititz Moravian congregation names visitors who came to see Tannenberg's new organ, but it does not give the place for which the organ was made.

1773　Lebanon, Pennsylvania. For the chapel of Hebron Moravian congregation in South Lebanon Township, near the city of Lebanon.

1774 Lancaster, Pennsylvania. For Trinity Lutheran Church. The organ was replaced in 1854, but the case—somewhat enlarged—remains in the church.

1775 Lancaster, Pennsylvania. For St. Mary's Roman Catholic Church. First Reformed Church United Church of Christ in Lancaster now has the case from a small, four-stop organ that is thought to be from the organ built for St. Mary's Church.

1775 Frederick, Maryland. For the Evangelical Lutheran Church.

1776 Easton, Pennsylvania. For the union church, Lutheran and Reformed.

1776 Bethlehem, Pennsylvania. For the chapel of the Single Brothers' House. The organ was later moved to Nazareth, Pennsylvania, and is now in the Moravian Historical Society's Whitefield House in Nazareth.

1777 Lititz, Pennsylvania. For the chapel of the Single Brothers' House.

1780 York, Pennsylvania. For "Mr. Fischer," presumably John Fischer, a York clockmaker, wood-carver, and portrait painter.

1782 Hope, Warren County, New Jersey. For the chapel of the Moravian congregation.

1783 Hagerstown, Maryland. Probably for either St. John's Lutheran Church in Hagerstown or St. Peter's (Beards) Lutheran Church near Hagerstown.

1784 York, Pennsylvania. For the German Reformed Church.

1786 Egypt, Whitehall Township, Lehigh County, Pennsylvania. For the union church, Lutheran and Reformed.

1787 Lititz, Pennsylvania. For the Moravian Church.

1790 Philadelphia, Pennsylvania. For Zion Lutheran Church.

1791 Spring City, East Pikeland Township, Chester County, Pennsylvania. For Zion Lutheran Church.

1793 Graceham, Frederick County, Maryland. For the Moravian Church. The organ is now in the parlor of the Single Brothers' House in Lititz, Pennsylvania.

1793 *Nazareth, Pennsylvania. For the chapel of the Moravian congre-gation in Nazareth Hall but later transferred to a new church build-ing. The organ was replaced in 1913, but the Tannenberg case—somewhat enlarged—and three of the Tannenberg stops were retained.*

By 1795 Philadelphia, Pennsylvania. For the German Reformed Church.

1795 "Guts'town." The location of this organ is uncertain.

1795 (or possibly 1789) Lower Heidelberg Township, Berks Coun-ty, Pennsylvania. For St. John's (Hain's) German Reformed Church.

1796 Baltimore, Maryland. For Zion Lutheran Church.

1797 "Macungie," Pennsylvania. Probably for either Ziegel Union Church, Lutheran and Reformed, Weisenberg Township, Lehigh County, or Zion's (Lehigh) Lutheran Church, Lowes Macungie Township, Lehigh County.

By 1798 Tohickon, Bedminster Township, Bucks County, Pennsyl-vania. For the union church, Lutheran and Reformed (now St. Peter's United Church of Christ and Peace Lutheran Church).

1798 *Salem (now Winston-Salem), North Carolina. For the chapel of the Moravian congregation. The organ is now in the chapel of the Single Brothers' House in Old Salem.*

1798 Lititz, Pennsylvania. For the chapel of the Single Sisters' House.

1799 Lancaster, Pennsylvania. For the Moravian Church.

1799 "Witepain" [Whitpain] Township, Montgomery County, Pennsylvania. For St. John's Lutheran Church, Center Square.

1800 *Salem (now Winston-Salem), North Carolina. For the Mora-vian Church. The organ has been newly installed in the auditorium of the Old Salem Visitor Center.*

1801 New Holland, Pennsylvania. For St. Stephen German Reformed Church.

1802 *Madison, Virginia. For Hebron Evangelical Lutheran Church.*

1804 *York, Pennsylvania. For Christ Lutheran Church. The organ is now in the York County Heritage Trust's Historical Society Museum in York.*[11]

William H. Armstrong is the author of *Organs for America: The Life and Work of David Tannenberg* (Philadelphia: University of Pennsylvania Press, 1967).

ENDNOTES

1. Herbert H. Beck, "Town Regulations of Lititz, 1759." *Papers Read Before the Lancaster County Historical Society,* 39, no. 5 (1935): 111.

2. Bethlehem Moravian Elders' Conference, November 19, 1781, the Moravian Archives, Bethlehem, Pennsylvania.

3. *Pennsylvania Gazette,* January 10, 1771, quoted in Paul E. Beck, "David Tanneberger, Organ Builder." *Papers Read Before the Lancaster County Historical Society,* 30, no. 1 (1926): 5.

4. Thomas Anburey, *Travels Through the Interior Parts of America.* 2 vols. (Boston: Houghton Mifflin, 1923), 2:176–77.

5. Abraham R. Beck, "Extracts from the Brethren's House and Congregational Diaries of the Moravian Church at Lititz, Pennsylvania, Relating to the Revolutionary War." *The Penn Germania,* 1, nos. 11–12 (November–December 1912): 849.

6. Ibid, 852.

7. Lititz Moravian Elders' Conference, October 30, 1779, the Moravian Archives, Bethlehem, Pennsylvania.

8. *Neue Philadelphische Correspondenz* (Philadelphia), no. 4, October 12, 1790.

9. *Philadelphia Gazette,* January 7, 1795; William Guthrie, *A New System of Modern Geography.* 2 vols. (Philadelphia: Mathew Carey, 1795), 2:447.

10. *Journals of the House of Representatives of the Commonwealth of Pennsylvania, November 28, 1776–October 2, 1781* (Philadelphia: J. Dunlap, 1782), 1:117–122.

11. In addition to making, tuning, and repairing organs, Tannenberg is known to have made at least two pianos and a clavicembalo (a kind of harpsichord), and to have prepared plans for the building of a clavichord.

SOURCES

The source for most of this essay on Tannenberg's life is the author's book, *Organs for America: The Life and Work of David Tannenberg.* The author has also benefited from more recent studies, especially Raymond J. Brunner, *"That Ingenious Business": Pennsylvania German Organ Builders* (Birdsboro, PA: The Pennsylvania German Society, 1990) and Carol A. Traupman-Carr, ed., *"Pleasing for Our Use": David Tannenberg and the Organs of the Moravians* (Bethlehem, PA: Lehigh University Press, 2000).

"... one of the finest instruments I have made ..."

The Home Moravian Church Tannenberg Organ

PAULA LOCKLAIR

"The road continues good . . . to Salem. . . . The first view of the town is romantic, just as it breaks upon you through the woods; it is pleasantly seated on a rising ground, and is surrounded by beautiful meadows, well-cultivated fields, and shady woods . . . Between eight and nine o'clock I attended their evening service, which consisted only of singing, accompanied by an organ. I was very much pleased with the music, which was good. . . ."[1]

❧

To ACHIEVE A GOOD QUALITY OF LIFE is a recurring theme in the written Moravian records, and music was an important element of daily life that helped define the high quality. Paul Larson succinctly explains this role of music in Moravian communities in his book, *An American Musical Dynasty:*

FIGURE 1. *A View of Salem in N. Carolina* by Ludwig Gottfried von Redeken, 1787. *Collection of the Wachovia Historical Society (acc. P-537), photograph by Old Salem Inc.*

. . . the Brethren believed that music directly influenced character. Words were the language of the mind, but music was the language of the soul. God spoke to humans through sacred texts, but He communicated with the soul through music . . . Moravians also held that music was a powerful way to embed religious beliefs in people's minds, because verses were easily memorized when they were sung. As a result, music was particularly important in teaching young children how to read. After they learned the alphabet, they spelled words from the Scriptures, from hymns, and from the Daily Text for children.[2]

Music was an essential element in all Moravian worship services. There were many services conducted throughout the week, and music was necessary to each one. In addition to hearing music and participating in church services, for an additional fee, young people in the boys' and girls' schools could receive music instruction. Some of the boys and girls of Wachovia would later become accomplished musicians, some as church organists; and some of the boys, as young men, would serve as "bellows pushers," or *calcants,* for the Salem church's organ bellows.

The congregation town of Salem was planned, built, and administered by the Moravian Church. It was the Moravians' third and primary settlement in a tract of nearly 100,000 acres in the North Carolina Backcountry that they called Wachovia. This land was purchased by the church in 1753 from John Carteret, the Earl of Granville, a Proprietor of the Royal Province of North Carolina. The Moravians had established two other towns in Wachovia before Salem: Bethabara (1753) and Bethania (1759). By the early 1770s, three more country congregations were being developed: Friedberg, Friedland, and Hope.

Salem was to be the primary town and serve as the religious and economic center of Wachovia. Its construction began in 1766, and it was ready for habitation by the spring of 1772, when 120 men, women, and children moved from Bethabara to Salem. Together they forged a vibrant and successful town where the musical traditions of Bethabara were continued.

The first musical instrument mentioned in the Moravian records for Wachovia is a trumpet at Bethabara in February 1754, only three months after the arrival of the first group of settlers. The next year flutes and a French horn were added, followed by two violins in 1756 and a "cabinet organ" in 1762.[3] This organ was probably built in Pennsylvania by organ builders Johann Gottlob Klemm and David Tannenberg. The excitement the organ's arrival created was recorded in the Bethabara Diary on July 8, 1762: "Br. Graff set up in our Saal [prayer hall or chapel] the organ he brought from Bethlehem; and during the Singstunde [song service] in the evening we heard an organ played for the first time in Carolina, and were very happy and

FIGURE 2. Joseph Bulitschek's 1773 organ built for the Saal in Bethania, North Carolina. *Old Salem Photographic Archives, S-19.*

thankful that it had reached us safely."[4] Many years later, in the 1790s, Tannenberg would build two more organs for the North Carolina Moravians, this time for Salem, and with the assistance of his son-in-law, Philip Bachmann.

In 1771, one of Tannenberg's apprentices, Joseph Ferdinand Bulitschek (1729–1801), moved from Lititz, Pennsylvania, to Wachovia and settled in Bethania, where he practiced the trades of millwright, cabinetmaker, and organ builder. Almost immediately after his arrival in Bethania he was asked to propose a plan for an organ for the Saal in Salem's new *Gemein Haus* (congregation house). This instrument, with two stops, was completed in October of 1772. He finished a second two-stop organ, for the Saal in Bethania, not quite a year later, in September 1773.[5] There are no further records that Bulitschek built organs, but it is documented that he did do some organ tuning.

Bulitschek's organ served Salem well for over twenty years, but in 1794 it was decided that a new organ was needed for the Gemein Haus. The Salem Board Minutes for June 19 recorded: "Our organ is in bad condition, and is affecting the singing and the instrumental music. We have long wished for a new one, and Council resolved to order one without further delay."[6] After much correspondence and negotiations with David Tannenberg, and the ensuing delays, the new one-manual organ was finally ready in the spring of 1798. Tannenberg was seventy years old at that time and long distance travel was difficult for him. Because of this he sent Philip Bachmann to in-

FIGURE 3. The Moravian Gemein Haus in Salem, North Carolina, c. 1856.
Courtesy of Moravian Archives, Winston-Salem, North Carolina.

stall the organ. The organ arrived on May 7, 1798. It was set up in the Gemein Haus Saal by Bachmann and played for the first time on May 22.[7]

Because the Bulitschek organ was still usable, it was sold to the Bethabara Congregation. Bachmann moved it, set it up in the Saal at Bethabara, and tuned it on May 23, 1798.[8] The original 1762 "little organ" was bought by Salem's Single Brethren and moved from Bethabara and installed as the first organ in the Saal in the Single Brothers' House in Salem.[9] This change was probably made because the Bulitschek organ was a larger instrument, which could serve the Bethabara congregation better. The "little organ" remained in the Single Brothers' Saal until the Salem congregation gave it to the Friedberg congregation for their new church in 1823, after the Salem Single Brothers closed their choir house. The ultimate fate of this organ is unknown.

The Salem congregation had a long wait for the new organ for their Gemein Haus, but it apparently was very satisfactory, because during the spring of 1798 while Bachmann was still in Salem, there were discussions with him, and with Tannenberg via letter, about ordering a new, large organ from Tannenberg for Salem's new church, then in the planning stages. It was decided to have an organ with two manuals and pedals. The location within the church was undecided, however, and that question was submitted to the Lot.[10] The published Elders Conference Minutes record that the Lot that was drawn, said: "The Saviour approves that plans be made to place the organ in the new church in the gallery on the steeple side." The Minutes then continue: "Under these circumstances we think that the church should be made as much longer and wider as possible."[11] A further explanation is found in the unpublished portion of these Minutes. Here it is recorded that the suggestion to locate the organ on the steeple side was made because "it was thought the music would sound out better." But because this arrangement would mean omitting the "choir," or balcony, opposite the minister, some seating would be lost.[12] Thus the seating problem could be solved by increasing the size of the church.

Ground was broken for the church by the end of May 1798 and the next month, on June 12th, the cornerstone was set. The following year, in November 1799, Philip Bachmann returned to Salem with one of the windchests for the organ as well as "other parts of our organ made in Lititz."[13] Tannenberg wrote in a letter that he had provided Bachmann "insofar as possible, with all the necessary sketches and instructions . . . I ask only that he be helped in every possible way . . . For my part I still have a full load of work here with the tin pipes and the lattice work."[14] Bachmann worked with cabinetmakers Jacob Fetter[15] and Joseph Leinbach to build the case for the organ and with Christoph Vogler for "Smithswork."[16] The decision of how to pump the three large organ bellows—which were to be located in the church attic above the organ—was also left up to Bachmann. The choice was for either treading or for pulling the bellows, and treading was chosen. Originally the treading was done in the attic, but this was changed in October 1802 so that the treading was done in the organ gallery.[17] This location, which allowed better communication between the organist and the person treading the bellows, was used until the organ was dismantled in 1910.

The other two windchests were apparently finished by June 1800 when Tannenberg wrote to Samuel Stotz in Salem that he had borrowed the local store scales and that one windchest weighed 444 pounds and the other 560 pounds. He also said, "I have made every possible effort to pack the pipes well so that they may reach you undamaged." Perhaps Tannenberg's strongest statement about this organ occurs in this same letter when he said, "I am indeed certain that if everything is done according to the plan, the result will be one of the finest instruments I have made or designed."[18]

David Tannenberg lamented throughout the building of this organ that he could not be in Salem, and as the time of completion drew closer, he was even more specific. On October 17, 1800, less

FIGURE 4. The bellows for Tannenberg's 1800 organ in the attic of Home Moravian Church. *Old Salem Photographic Archives, S-2246.*

FIGURE 5.
Tannenberg's 1798
organ built for the
Gemein Haus in Salem,
North Carolina. *Collection of the Wachovia Historical Society (acc. O-1), photograph by Old Salem Inc., S-622.*

than a month before the dedication of the new church, he wrote to the administrator of Salem, Frederic William Marshall:

I am very sorry that I could not have the pleasure . . . to see you in person, notwithstanding that I tried everything to so do. Yes, even my second marriage was for this purpose, that if I would leave here, I would have somebody in my house in whom I had confidence and would not be compelled to put somebody else in it or even to close it up. But because this was delayed longer than I expected and also more and more scruples made themselves felt about my leaving and even more about my return trip, which would have taken place in wintertime, so I finally lost courage. . . .[19]

He also regretted not being there to help Bachmann because "the inserting and tuning is so much work for one person and cannot be shortened especially since the installing and tuning takes so much time and requires effort and patience which he (Bachmann) might lack at times."[20]

The construction of the church took a year and a half, and it was consecrated on November 9, 1800, with about 2000 people in attendance. At that time the Wachovia Memorabilia records that, "we thanked the Lord for the successful completion of our church . . . thanked Him also for our organ. . . ."[21]

The organist for this service was probably Gottlieb Schober (1756–1838). Br. Schober came to Wachovia from Bethlehem, Pennsylvania, in 1769, when he was thirteen years old. His early education at Nazareth Hall, a Moravian boarding school for boys in Nazareth, Pennsylvania, must have included organ lessons, as the Bethabara Diary for March 2, 1770, records that: "The little Schober played the cabinet organ for the first time, for the singing of the liturgy "O Head so full of bruises."[22] His interest in the organ continued, and in July 1790 he was asked to be one of three Salem organists to play for worship services. The three organists would rotate weekly.[23] Schober became even move involved in Salem's musical history when he supervised the arrangements for the acquisition of David Tannenberg's first organ for Salem in 1794. Gottlieb Schober became a prominent and distinguished citizen, as well as an accomplished musician, so it

FIGURE 6. Detail from *Church and Inspectors House at Salem, NC*, c. 1840, by Gustavus Grunewald (1805–1878) and Peter S. Duval. *Collection of the Wachovia Historical Society (acc. P-318), photograph by Old Salem Inc., S-286.*

FIGURE 7. Tannenberg's wax seal. *Collection of Old Salem Inc., acc. 4438.*

is not surprising that he was appointed the supervisor of musicians and placed in charge of the music in 1799. In this capacity he was also very likely the organist who played for the dedication of the church. His interests in the organ continued, as shown by his request in 1804 to fellow musician, Johann Friedrich Peter, in Pennsylvania, that Peter copy for him "an organ voice to Graun's 'Te Deum.'"[24]

❧

Philip Bachmann arrived back in Lititz by early December 1800. David Tannenberg had expected him to stay in Salem for a while and make any necessary adjustments to the organ, including additional tuning. This is clear in a letter Tannenberg wrote to Samuel Stotz in which he said:

[Bachmann] assured me that he had done all he could [about the organ], but that there was nothing reliable to count on in the changeable *Clima.* This, of course, is true. Nevertheless, you can hope that the *Orgel* will become better from year to year as it becomes more accustomed to the *Clima.* But it should be thoroughly tuned now and then over a period of time until you have no more trouble. At first a new instrument changes often and in great measure . . . You can still improve it from time to time in regard to tuning, and the like. The main part was made here under my supervision, and the tin pipes are altogether my handiwork. . . .[25]

There seem to have been some questions about the total cost of the Home Church organ, the payments to Tannenberg, and the accounting of Bachmann's expenses.[26] It is not clear how this was resolved, but Tannenberg wrote that he was concerned about the cost from the beginning: "I saw in advance that it would be expensive for you and did not readily accept [the order]. But I considered what it would cost you to get one from Europe, also at great risk and expense. And so I *Resolvirte* to take on the work. . . ."[27]

The issues of the proper tuning of the organ and the final payments were still being discussed by Tannenberg in letters to Samuel Stotz in 1802. On May 25th, Tannenberg wrote again about settling the payments and still wanting an account of what Bachmann paid to craftsmen who had assisted him in Salem. But the main purpose of the letter was to send a detailed description of how to tune an organ, as apparently Bachmann left Salem before teaching anyone the fine art of tuning. At the very end of his instructions, Tannenberg writes:

At this point, the chiefest thing I can note in regard to tuning an organ is, of course, that it calls for long experience. Indeed, I should not have left Salem without having had a Brother present to watch and listen while I set up and tuned the whole thing . . . Anyhow, the main thing is to be sure not to deviate from the general tone prevailing in the organ. Thus no organ goes very far out of tune.[28]

The organ, which was first heard in 1800 during the services to dedicate the church, continued to be an attraction. There apparently were many requests for the organ to be played for visitors to Salem, and on May 18, 1803, the *Aeltesten Conferenz* [Elders Conference] noted in their minutes that a "box has been put on the organ into which outsiders for whom it is played can put something."[29]

Most of the visitors to Salem spoke either English or German, but occasionally Cherokee Indians came through Salem. In 1806 three Indians, who had been to the country's capital, Washington, stopped in Salem on their way home. Even though they spoke neither English nor German, music proved to be the common method of communication as "the Indians especially enjoyed the singing of the children and the boarding pupils, first in the Boarding School to the accompaniment of a pianoforte, and then in the church where the members of the Aeltesten Conferenz and others met them, and the organ was played for the singing."[30]

In 1809 William D. Martin made a trip from South Carolina to Connecticut. Along the way he stopped in Salem, and he described the town in detail, including the church. "Their church is large &

magnificent. In its steeple is a bell, which strikes the hours, as also, each quarter sufficiently loud to be heard distantly through the town. They have a very large, & I should presume, a good organ."[31]

While the organ was used primarily for church services for the Salem congregation, frequently special services were also held. For instance, in 1808 a group of fifteen Methodist preachers, who were about to be ordained deacons, visited Salem along with "a fairly large number of Methodists and people of other persuasions." The preachers all wanted to attend the Moravian church service, and requested that it be held in English. A Singstunde was held using the English Hymn Book, and a large number of Salem residents and all of the Girls' Boarding School students also attended. "The singing was especially sweet, hearty and pleasing, and the preachers listened with reverence and emotion, and said afterwards how much they had enjoyed the meaning of the stanzas, the singing itself, and the organ accompaniment. Some were moved even to tears."[32]

The Moravians wanted to be able to communicate through music to their English-speaking guests. This was particularly clear in 1790:

Only a few compositions which have German words lend themselves well to English, so perhaps several English compositions might be ordered from Pennsylvania. The anthem: *O dass Ihn doch jedes mit frölichem Geiste,* has the same scansion in English as in German and will serve as an example. The use of anthems with English text is especially recommended when officials of state or nation are present.[33]

This piece called for four voice parts, two horns, two violins, a viola, violoncello, and an organ. The German language continued to dominate Salem until mid-century. After a low attendance for services on "Ascension day" in 1857 the Salem Diary recorded, "Liturgies in the German language have seen their day here at Salem and ought to be abolished altogether."[34]

As has been previously explained, the organ could not be played without two people: the organist and "bellows pusher," or calcant. Just a month after the church's dedication, the *Aufseher Collegium* (Board of Supervisors) began trying to find young men who would commit to the "office" of bellows pusher. This person needed to be present not only for services, but also for all practice sessions. It was thought that four or five Brethren would be best so that they could rotate on a weekly basis. By Christmas of 1800, five young men had agreed: John Buttner, a potter, age twenty-two; Jesse Buttner, John's brother, a blacksmith, age twenty-four; Van Neman Zevely, an apprentice in the Single Brothers' joinery, age twenty; Christian Schulz, a shoemaker's apprentice, age seventeen; and Peter Oliver, a free African American potter, age thirty-four. As long as the organ was in service, there was a continual need for bellows pushers as well as organists.

The church did not designate an official position of "Church Organist" until the late 1850s. From the time of the first organ in Bethabara in 1762 until the late nineteenth century, a great variety of musicians played the organs for church services in Wachovia. These organists often were rather itinerant and played for services in Salem, Bethabara, Bethania, and Friedberg.

In his book, *An American Musical Dynasty,* Paul Larson ably describes the role of the Moravian organist:

Though there were many Moravian composers who played the organ, they created no distinctive body of literature for the instrument, for the Moravian use of the organ was unique. Christian Ignatius Latrobe, the most influential eighteenth-century Moravian musical spokesman, described the uniqueness in the preface to his chorale book. "To be able to play a voluntary [solo organ piece] is by no means an essential part of the qualifications of an organist among the Brethren. The congregation will often prefer hearing Hymn-tunes in its stead." Rather than playing extended preludes, offertories, and postludes, Moravian organists led congregational singing, kept the pitch of the hymns, and were part of the *collegium musicum.* While the Moravian organists did not indulge in display, great demands were placed upon their memories and upon their improvisational skills.[35]

The Singstunde was a frequent Moravian service. The unannounced hymns, which provided the theme or lesson for the service, were selected by the pastor, who began the singing. The organist needed to be able to play any tune in any key and accompany the congregation. Larson also described this talent:

The organist should be able to play the Hymn-tunes in most, if not all, of the different keys extempore; because, upon many occasions, the verses sung by the minister, according to his own choice, are taken from a variety of hymns, and it would be next to impossible to turn continually to the Tune-book, without detriment to the singing; especially as such single verses are often given out, or sung, without previous notice, he may assist the weak singer, . . . if left to his choice, or in the key the singer himself pitches upon.[36]

The vast majority of organists in Wachovia seem to have been men, but in 1823 the Bethania Diary records that their organist was Sr. Johanna Elisabeth Oehman. There are also mentions in Salem records of pupils at both the Girls' Boarding School and the Boys' School taking organ lessons, and these students often had their first experiences playing for a congregation when they played for the services for their school.

The Home Church organ underwent routine maintenance and tuning during the nineteenth century. The first major alteration was in 1845 when "2 swell boxes for the large organ" were added, apparently made by Salem cabinetmakers Jacob and John Siewers.[37] This was probably under the instruction of George J. Corrie of Philadelphia, whom the Salem Congregation paid for thirty-eight days of work for "tuning and repairing two church organs."[38]

The next major work on the organ was twenty-five years later, in 1870, when William Schwarze, a representative of Henry Erben, a New York organ builder, spent thirty full days and twenty-two half days making alterations to the organ. Also at this time the interior of the church received its first renovation, and the sanctuary was not used between August 14, 1870, and December 23, 1870. The first service in the remodeled sanctuary, with the refurbished organ, was Christmas Eve 1870. The Salem Diary recorded:

The organ has been greatly improved by the work done upon it. All the pipes were taken out & repairing done wherever necessary, some addition-

FIGURE 8. c. 1870 view of the interior of Home Moravian Church and the Tannenberg organ. *Collection of Old Salem Inc., acc. 4270.5, S-18010.*

al stops or registers were put in, and the pitch lowered, as it had been too high. The woodwork was grained in walnut, to correspond with the pulpit and the whole appearance of the instrument is much improved thereby.[39]

The organ continued to be used consistently over the next forty years for regular services and special occasions, such as the "Fiftieth Anniversary" celebration for the Rt. Rev. Edward Rondthaler on July 24, 1892. "The day was very warm . . . an immense congregation filled the church. At the stroke of the clock the organ pealed forth a joyful voluntary, as the Bishop accompanied by the other ministers, entered and occupied the places on the platform . . . A special Jubilee Ode had been prepared."[40]

But sadly the Home Church Diary for June 24, 1910, records:

The old organ, which for more than a century has done such splendid service in the Home Church, was removed today and stored in the Garret of the Salem Boys School. For some months it has been realized that it had served its day and could not again be repaired satisfactorily.[41]

This began another remodeling of the church interior, and it re-opened with services and a new "tubular pneumatic instrument . . . built by the well-known Kimball Company, of Chicago" on November 30, 1913.[42]

Fortunately, the historical importance of David Tannenberg's organ for the Salem Moravian Church was recognized at the time of its dismantling and it was not destroyed, but it remained in storage in various locations for eighty-eight years. Since the restoration began in 1998, nearly two hundred years of this organ's history have been deciphered and analyzed by Taylor & Boody Organbuilders of Staunton, Virginia. With meticulous care and understanding, the organ has been returned to its original state, musically and visually, and it stands as a tribute to the talent and craftsmanship of master organ builder, David Tannenberg, his able assistant and son-in-law, Philip Bachmann, and the various Salem craftsmen who willingly worked alongside Bachmann to complete a remarkable musical achievement in the North Carolina Backcountry.

Paula Locklair is Vice President of MESDA and the Horton Center Museums at Old Salem Inc., co-author with John Bivins Jr. of *Moravian Decorative Arts in North Carolina* (Winston-Salem, NC: Old Salem Inc., 1981), and author of *Quilts, Coverlets, and Counterpanes* (Winston-Salem, NC: Old Salem Inc., 1997).

ENDNOTES

1. "Journal of William Loughton Smith, 1790-1791," in *Massachusetts Historical Society: Proceedings* (Boston, 1918), vol. LI, , 73, 74.

2. Paul S. Larson, *An American Musical Dynasty: A Biography of the Wolle Family of Bethlehem, Pennsylvania* (Bethlehem, PA: Lehigh University Press, 2002), 28.

3. Dr. Adelaide L. Fries, *Records of the Moravians in North Carolina* (Raleigh: North Carolina Historical Commission, 1943), vol. I, 241, 247, 411.

4. Ibid, vol. I, 247.

5. This organ survived until it was destroyed in a fire on November 3, 1942. Tannenberg supplied the pipes for a third stop for this organ in October 1800.

6. Fries, *Records,* vol. VI, 2508.

7. Ibid, vol. VI, 2605.

8. Ibid, vol. VI, 2615.

9. Ibid, vol. VI, 2605.

10. "The Moravians used the Lot to determine God's will in spiritual and secular matters . . . Only the church board of elders was authorized to use it . . . After the elders had done everything possible to reach a sound conclusion about what should be done in a matter . . . two or three outcomes, or Lots, were written on slips of paper, encased in slender tubes cut from reeds, and place in the Lot bowl . . . One Lot was then solemnly drawn from the bowl, and the answer it gave was heeded." From Penelope Niven, *Old Salem: The Official Guidebook* (Winston-Salem, NC: Old Salem), 23.

11. Fries, *Records,* vol. VI, 2611.

12. Minutes of the Elders' Conference, May 17, 1798, Moravian Archives, Southern Province, Winston-Salem, North Carolina.

13. Fries, *Records,* vol. VI, 2627.

14. Letter from David Tannenberg to Samuel Stotz, November 13, 1799, Moravian Music Foundation.

15. Jacob Fetter came to Salem from Bethlehem, Pennsylvania, at the same time as Bachmann, but he was to stay in Salem. Fries, *Records,* vol. VI, 2627.

16. Ibid. vol. VI, 2631 and *Journal No. II, Salem Diacony, May 1st 1800–April 30th 1807,* September 23 to October 18, 1800 (Winston-Salem, NC: Moravian Archives Southern Province).

17. Fries, *Records,* vol. VI, 2703.

18. Letter from David Tannenberg to Samuel Stotz, June 11, 1800. Moravian Music Foundation.

19. Letter from David Tannenberg to Frederick William Marshall, October 17, 1800, Moravian Music Foundation.

20. Ibid.

21. Fries, *Records,* vol. VI, 2639.

22. Ibid, vol. I, 411.

23. Ibid, vol. V, 2308. The other two organists were Brs. Ruez and Meinung.

24. Letter from Johann Friedrich Peter to Gottlieb Schober, September 8, 1804. Schober Papers, Old Salem Library, Winston-Salem, North Carolina. Peter was Salem's music director from 1780–1790 and was the most famous eighteenth century Moravian American composer.

25. Letter from David Tannenberg to Samuel Stotz, December 7, 1800. Moravian Music Foundation.

26. "The Salem congregation ledger shows £5785:6:0 as the cost of the church, with an additional £794:9:10 for the organ . . ." Fries, *Records,* vol. VII, 2655.

27. Letter from David Tannenberg to Samuel Stotz, December 7, 1800.

28. Letter from David Tannenberg to Samuel Stotz, May 25, 1802. Moravian Music Foundation. For a published translation of Tannenberg's tuning instructions see *Moravian Music Journal,* vol. 31, no. 2 (Fall 1986).

29. Fries, *Records,* vol. VI, 2742.

30. Ibid, vol. VI, 2846.

31. Anna D. Elmore, The Journal of William Martin (Charlotte, NC: Heritage House, 1959), 12. William Martin was traveling from Edgefield, South Carolina, to Litchfield, Connecticut, to study law. He later was elected to the United States Congress from South Carolina.

32. Fries, Records, vol. VI, 2915.

33. Ibid, vol. V, 2308.

34. C. Daniel Crews and Lisa D. Bailey, eds., *Records of the Moravians in North Carolina* (Raleigh, North Carolina Division of Archives and History, 2000), vol. XII, 6227.

35. Larson, *An American Musical Dynasty,* 39. Larson defines the collegium musicum as "the instrumental group that provided sacred instrumental music along with the trombone choir" (29).

36. Ibid, 40.

37. "Thomas Pfohl in act with J & J Siewers, 1845 Dec. 4th.," "Bills and Receipts" file, Moravian Archives, Southern Province, Winston-Salem, North Carolina. The "swell boxes" cost $25.00. Brothers Jacob Friedrich and John Daniel Siewers went into the cabinetmaking business together in 1842.

38. Salem Diacony Journal, December 1845, 320, Moravian Archives, Southern Province, Winston-Salem, North Carolina.

39. Salem Diary, December 24, 1870, Moravian Archives, Southern Province, Winston-Salem, North Carolina.

40. J.H. Clewell, comp., *Jubilee Celebration of the Rt. Rev. Edward Rondthaler, D.D.* (Salem, NC, 1893). Located in the Jane Welfare Papers, Old Salem Collection, Winston-Salem, North Carolina.

41. Home Church Diary, June 24, 1910, Moravian Archives, Southern Province, Winston-Salem, North Carolina.

42. From a Winston-Salem, North Carolina, newspaper, November 1913. This is found in the Wachovia Historical Society Scrapbook #2, in the Old Salem Research Center, Winston-Salem, North Carolina.

The Restoration of the Home Moravian Church Tannenberg Organ

BRUCE SHULL

The restoration of the 1800 Tannenberg organ built for Home Moravian Church in Salem, North Carolina, began in essence with the decision to keep the old instrument and store it in the church attic when it was disassembled and removed from the sanctuary in 1910. One can only guess as to the thinking that preserved the organ parts rather than simply throwing them out. Perhaps the high quality of the workmanship spoke to those charged with dismantling the old organ and they could neither bring themselves to destroy nor discard the instrument. It seems likely that none of the people involved with the dismantling and storage of the organ in 1910 could have imagined that over the next ninety-four years the organ would lie in pieces and be moved countless times and then be meticulously documented and restored. Little could they have known that the organ would again one day be a prized possession and an invaluable artifact.

FIGURE 1. Photo of the Tannenberg organ and church interior decorated for the 100th anniversary of the church building and organ in 1900. This photo shows the organ in its last configuration before its removal from the church in 1910. *Collection of the Wachovia Historical Society (acc. 4021.265), photograph by Old Salem Inc., S-19500.*

The Organ Case

The case of this organ is one example among several surviving Tannenberg instruments with cases that were made outside of his Lititz, Pennsylvania, workshop. It is the largest surviving case that still houses a complete Tannenberg organ.

The case was made in Salem by Tannenberg's son-in-law, Philip Bachmann, no doubt to save costs and avoid the shipping of more large parts than necessary from Pennsylvania to North Carolina. An eighteen-year old joinery apprentice, Jacob Fetter, assisted Bachmann with the case construction. Since the case was built on-site, the Salem organ could not have been set up as a complete unit in Tannenberg's workshop. In fact, the trackers and stop rod traces as well as other parts would have had to have been cut to length and fitted to the organ in North Carolina. This would not have been an unusual situation for organ builders of Tannenberg's training or experience. It is interesting to speculate whether or not the pipes were played on the windchests in Tannenberg's workshop. Records appear to indicate that Bachmann traveled to Salem bringing along the completed windchests when he began his eleven-month stay there. The pipes must have been voiced in the shop but many would undoubtedly have required some straightening and revoicing after their long trip from Pennsylvania.

The façade design is typical of Tannenberg's later organs. There is a large central tower with a rounded front housing the bass pipes of the Principal 8′. The largest Principal pipe in the façade is D. C and C sharp are located inside the case and are stopped wooden pipes. The tenor pipes of the Principal are housed in the two towers that also have semi-circular projections at the outer edges of the case. The two flat pipe fields between the towers house the lower treble pipes of the Principal and also in this case are the bottom four notes of the Principal Octav 4′. The case moldings are classical in origin and the fluted front stiles add a look of refinement to the composi-

FIGURE 2. The earliest known photo of the Tannenberg organ in Home Moravian Church. The presence of the gas light fixtures throughout the room and on the organ date the photo to c. 1860. The balcony shape and configuration are likely the original for the church and organ. The need for the projection in the balcony railing for the organ console was mentioned in church records at the time of the church construction. *Collection of the Wachovia Historical Society (acc. 4021.267-268), photograph by Old Salem Inc., S-114.*

tion. The frames have molded edges and the raised portions in the center of the inset panels are faced to the inside of the case.

Microscopic analysis of the wood shows that the case was constructed primarily of southern yellow pine. The use of yellow pine is logical since the lumber, native to North Carolina, would have been readily available in Salem from the surrounding forests. It is significant to note that the upper section of the console and the moldings and tower turnings are made from tulip poplar. In Salem, both tulip poplar and yellow pine were used as secondary woods; and tulip poplar was a commonly used wood in Pennsylvania cabinet shops. The use of tulip poplar begs the question as to where the upper console and moldings and tower turnings were made: in Salem or in Tannenberg's workshop and then taken by Bachmann to North Carolina when he traveled there for the case construction and eventual organ setup? The large turnings for the towers with their included moldings would not necessarily have been constructed in Salem. In fact, it may have been easier to make them in Lititz and overcome the difficulties of transport to Salem because the workshop in Pennsylvania would likely have had a large faceplate lathe and the appropriate planes that Tannenberg had certainly acquired by that time for construction of earlier organs. It is unknown whether Salem craftsmen at that time would have had these specialized tools required to complete the moldings and tower turnings.

The casework of the organ has survived mostly intact; however, significant changes have been made to parts of the case. Slots were crudely cut into the side panels of the lower case when changes were made to allow the organ to be pumped from the gallery instead of the apparent original method of pumping it in the church attic where the bellows were housed. Similarly, crudely roughed-out holes were made in the cornice molding through which rods were passed to connect the pumping treadles to the levers beneath the bellows in the attic above. Changes to the Hinterwerk division included first two swell enclosures and later the addition of two stops of pipes. These alterations caused the interior back wall of the upper main

FIGURE 3. One of the corner joints of the impost before restoration. The joint was heavily damaged during the disassembly of the organ in 1910 due to the dovetail pins having been glued and wedged. *Photograph courtesy of Taylor & Boody Organbuilders.*

FIGURE 3A. Corner joint during restoration. The repairs were made using wood from reclaimed yellow pine beams. *Photograph courtesy of Taylor & Boody Organbuilders.*

FIGURE 3B. Restored corner joint of the impost. *Photograph courtesy of Taylor & Boody Organbuilders.*

case to be significantly changed and largely eliminated. Changes were also made to the side access doors on the organ case. Both doors were shortened and moved up and one was changed from swinging outward of the case to swinging inward. One set of the original hinges has been preserved.

The case construction involves typical mortise-and-tenon and dovetail joinery. It consists of a base frame topped by a lower case made up of vertical stiles and frames and panels. A large heavily constructed impost sits atop the lower case to which is added the upper case side panels and front stiles which in turn support the three large tower cornices. Most of the mortises are cut all the way through and the corresponding tenons are glued and wedged tightly in the mortises.

The half-blind dovetails holding the impost together were brutally forced apart during the 1910 disassembly of the organ as evidenced by the hammer marks on the inside of the impost. Since the case had been built on-site, it was not necessary to plan how to get the large assembled impost through doorways and into the church. Being more than ten feet square, the impost could not be removed from the church intact. The reason the joints came apart so reluctantly was discovered during the restoration of the organ. Kelley Blanton, head case-maker for Taylor & Boody Organbuilders, noticed after paint had been removed from the impost parts that the pins of the dovetail joints had been cut open with a handsaw. Likewise, the tails of the joints had been pared out in such a way that when wedges were driven into the slots in the pins the joint tightened up so that the joint behaved almost as if it were dovetailed in both directions. A normal dovetail joint can be pressed together in one direction while resisting pulling apart in the other direction. By wedging the tails, the joint is nearly as strong in terms of resisting separation in both directions. This type of construction has the added advantage that glue can be brushed into each joint in turn, after each has been pressed together without having to hurriedly assemble the entire unit while the glue is still wet. It also means that

FIGURE 4. An example of the wedged dovetails described in the text. These joints are on one of the upper cornice boxes of the case. The joint is very strong and would be extremely difficult if not impossible to disassemble. *Photograph courtesy of Taylor & Boody Organbuilders.*

the joint is self-clamping and that no large clamps are needed for assembling such a large structure.

The case of the organ was painted at least eight times during its 110-year tenure in Home Moravian Church. The original color was a slightly yellowed white for the bulk of the case with gold leaf applied to a gesso base on the carved pipe shades. The first repaintings of the case were carried out with only slight variations from the original color.

The fretwork screen atop the impost level is unique among the extant Tannenberg instruments and may have been something added by the case-makers to the original plan from Tannenberg. The screen was also originally gilded and the casework that is visible behind it was painted black.

Gaslights were added to the church around 1860 and two fixtures were attached to the organ on the front of each of the outer stiles. They are visible in the earliest known photograph of the organ. Holes were drilled through the base of the organ and through each of the two stiles for the gas supply pipes.

William Schwarze, the southern representative of Henry Erben, an organ building firm of New York, carried out a major rebuild of the organ in 1870. At this time the case was painted a dark brown and grained to resemble walnut. The gold leaf on the pipe shades and gallery fretwork were coated with bronze paint. Sometime around 1885 the organ was again repainted to harmonize with the current tastes in the decoration of the church interior. The lower case and console were grained to resemble quarter-sawn oak and the upper case was painted with various blues and grays and shades of aqua. Stenciling was done on the friezes between the cornice and lower moldings on the upper towers of the case. The façade pipes were also painted and stenciled.

It is noteworthy that, of the extant Tannenberg organs with ped-

FIGURE 5. Detail of the photograph presented as Figure 2. Visible in the photo are the windline running down the wall on the left side of the organ and the pumping rods extending from the ceiling down into the outermost tower on the right side of the organ. The pipe shade carvings and impost fretwork do not appear to be gilded by the time this photo was taken.

FIGURE 6. Photo of the Tannenberg organ as it appeared after the 1870 rebuilding. The case has been painted to resemble walnut. The windline visible to the left of the organ in earlier photographs had been moved by the time of this photo. The console top has a new molding and wooden fretwork decoration has been added to the sides of the console along the top edge of the balcony railing. *Collection of Old Salem Inc., acc.4270.5, S-18010 (detail).*

als, only this one has the Pedal division enclosed. The construction of the enclosure, formed by extending the organ base and impost and cornice moldings rearward and then fitting solid frame and panels below and frame and fretwork-pierced panels above, suggests that this too may have been somewhat of a modification of Tannenberg's design. It is important to note however, that the side moldings, which may have come from Tannenberg's Lititz workshop, were long enough to reach in one piece to the rear wall. Both the 1787 Lititz organ and the 1804 York organ have the same two-stop Pedal division and neither of these is enclosed. It is possible that someone (perhaps the church architect) didn't want to see the pedal pipes outside the case in the rear and successfully argued to have the case sides extended to cover these pipes and windchest.

There is compelling evidence that the main case, which houses the Hauptwerk and Hinterwerk divisions, originally had removable back panels on both the upper and lower cases. A large panel exists that covers the Pedal stop and playing actions vertically and one can also see where floorboards existed that covered the horizontal trackers and stop traces. Since the console back was integrated into the balcony railing and there was very little space between the console and the front of the case, it may be that the side access doors were used to provide a walkway through the organ from one side of the balcony to the other. The vertical cover over the pedal rollerboard and trackers would prevent damage to this delicate mechanism by people passing through the organ. This too would be a situation unique to this organ.

When Taylor & Boody Organbuilders set up the organ in Old Salem's Horton Center Gallery in 1998, it was discovered that numerous pieces of the case were missing. The two fluted front stiles of the lower case were nowhere to be found, as were all the toeboards for the façade pipes. All of the back panels and the back frame stiles that supported the rear of the center tower cornice had been removed from the organ during one of the several rebuildings of the organ and apparently discarded. Most troubling was the gradual re-

FIGURE 7. A c. 1885 photograph of the organ. The lower case has been grained to resemble quarter-sawn oak and the upper case painted in various colors. The façade pipes were painted and stenciled. The three pumping rods are clearly visible above the right tower of the organ but the slots through which they exit the ceiling have been elongated toward the right side of the organ. A large windline is visible just behind the three pumping rods. There is also an electric light hanging above the console and its switch is apparently mounted on the left stile of the center tower just above the impost. There are also hymn books and fans propped inside the gallery fretwork. This may explain why this fragile woodwork was found to be in such bad condition. *Old Salem Photographic Archives, S-115.*

FIGURE 8. Photo of the organ set up in 1998 in Old Salem's Horton Center Gallery. The flattened façade pipes could not be put into the organ. A single pipe however had been restored and is visible in the flat just to the right of the center tower. The console was originally installed against the balcony railing in the church and did not have a back of its own. This trial assembly of the organ paved the way for the planning of the organ's restoration. *Old Salem Photographic Archives, S-29955.*

alization that no signs of a floor frame or any other parts such as stop tree lower bearings that would have been originally attached to the gallery floor could be found. Was it possible that the workers disassembling the organ were intent on finishing the job and that changes planned for the gallery floor caused the organ's floor frame and other parts to be discarded? The lower molding skirt boards that were present had been coped and fitted to the floor of the gallery when the organ was installed as had been the case itself to the rear wall. All of these preserved case parts indicate that the gallery floor and the rear wall of the balcony had been anything but flat surfaces.

Playing Action

The playing action consists of the keyboards, trackers, square rails, and rollerboards. All of the original square rails and rollerboards have been preserved. The keyboards were replaced in 1870 during the rebuilding of the organ by Schwarze; however, the old Tannenberg key frames were retained and modified to fit the new keys. Aside from the new keys for both manuals and pedals, the remainder of the original playing action exists largely intact. Some roller arms and end pivot studs have been replaced over the years due to breakage. Trackers and tracker ends have similarly been repaired.

This organ is one of three remaining Tannenberg organs with a detached, reversed console. All three organs were built for Moravian churches. It is no coincidence that the Moravians regularly used the organ together with other instruments during the worship services. The reversed console clearly facilitated the organist's view of the other instrumentalists and conductor. This is the only extant Tannenberg organ with two manuals.

The supports for the rollerboards of the Hauptwerk and Hinterwerk divisions were sawn through, probably during the disassembly of the organ to aid in maneuvering the large rollerboards out of the case and through doorways.

The three large rollerboards for both manuals and pedal divisions are of yellow pine with yellow pine supports. This suggests that the fragile rollerboards may have been constructed in Salem perhaps using arms, bearings, and rollers made in Pennsylvania. The rollerboard supports are attached at the top to the windchest windbox bottoms and at the bottom to the floor. The rollers themselves are also of yellow pine and the roller arms and end bearing studs are of maple. The metal squares for the manuals are sawn from brass sheets and the edges have been filed. The squares for the Pedal division are made of maple. The squares are housed in wooden rails of cherry with an iron axle rod. The trackers are of tulip poplar with a soft iron wire inserted in each end and hammered flat into the tracker. The end joints were coated with hide glue and lashed with cotton thread held in place by the glue.

FIGURE 9. Pedal rollerboard and square rail before restoration. The restored pedal windchest sits atop the rollerboard supports. *Photograph courtesy of Taylor & Boody Organbuilders.*

The roller axles are iron and turn in the maple studs with no bushings. The ends of the axles are flush with the ends of the studs so that they cannot be easily removed. The axles also protrude into the roller far enough to pin in place the maple arms. The maple studs are drilled through the rollerboard and can be driven back through with a drift pin to remove them by cracking loose the hide glue joints. The maple roller arms also have no bushings for the tracker ends. The iron tracker wire ends are bent to go through the roller arms and brass squares. While this makes the action feel better to the organist, a certain amount of action noise when the organ is played is guaranteed by the metal-to-metal connections.

The Hauptwerk rollerboard has an additional set of rollers woven into its layout for the Hauptwerk-to-Pedal coupler. These rollers connect to pallets in the windchest at the top and to a set of wooden squares at the bottom. The wooden square rail can be slid forward or backward to contact a set of dogs on the horizontal pedal trackers to engage or disengage the coupler.

Stop Action

The stop action consists of the stop knobs and connecting rods, wooden trees inside the base of the console and main case, and forged iron rockers connected to the sliders inside the windchests. These sliders determine precisely which sets of pipes play or do not play when the organist depresses the keys.

Early in the study of the organ it was difficult to ascertain its original stoplist. The additions to the Hinterwerk windchest were obvious, but how had the organ been arranged originally stop-wise? In the course of scouring Moravian records for references to the Tan-

FIGURE 10. Original hand-forged stop action for the Hinterwerk-to-Hauptwerk coupler. The coupler actuator knob is housed in the left key cheek on the Hinterwerk keyframe. This is a rather sophisticated piece of engineering. *Photograph courtesy of Taylor & Boody Organbuilders.*

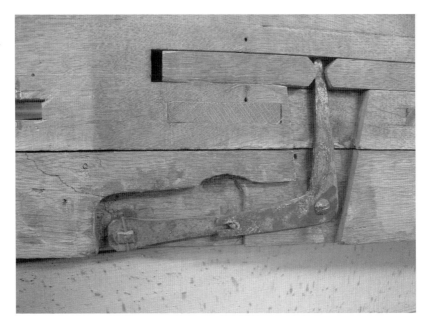

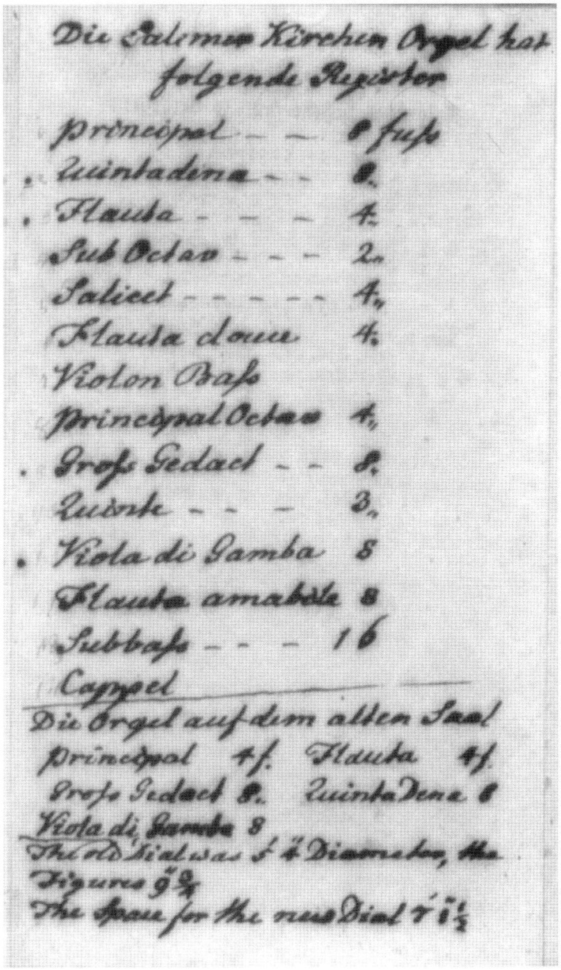

FIGURE 11. Photo of the page from the daily notebook of Frederic Marshall, administrator for the town of Salem where in 1801 he wrote down the stoplists for both of the Tannenberg organs. This information was invaluable both for restoring the proper pipes in each organ and for determining the order of the stops on the left and right stop jambs. *Courtesy of the Moravian Archives, Winston-Salem, North Carolina.*

nenberg organs, Old Salem's curator, Paula Locklair, found a notation in the daily notebook of Frederic Marshall, manager for the town of Salem, listing, incredibly enough, the stoplists for both the Home Church organ and the 1798 *Saal* (prayer hall or chapel) organ when they were nearly new. With this information, it was possible to determine which sets of pipes belonged to which organ. It was further discovered while the organ was set up for study in 1998 that Marshall had written the stops in the order that they were laid out down the stop jambs beginning with the side to the left of the organist. This proved to be invaluable information during the restoration of the organ.

Significant changes were made to the stop action, most notably during the 1870 rebuilding of the organ by Schwarze. Two stops were added to the organ at that time utilizing pipes of the Quintadena 8′ and Viola di Gamba 8′ from the organ built by Tannenberg in 1798 for Salem's Gemein Haus Saal. The addition of these stops in the form of an Open Diapason 8′ and a Picolo (sic) 2′ (these names were from Schwarze) on the Hinterwerk prompted some rearranging of the stops on the stop jambs, which further jumbled the stop trees and traces inside the case.

Other than moving some of the parts around, most of the stop action appears to have been preserved with the exception of some of the wooden connecting traces that were changed in length or replaced. Unfortunately, the original stop knobs were removed in the 1870 rebuild and apparently discarded. It now appears that no original stop knobs have been preserved on Tannenberg's extant organs with detached consoles.

Light pencil markings can be found on most of the oak stop trees with the stop names or abbreviations. When these notations have been found, they are at the top of the trees and frequently are accompanied by the notation "ob", perhaps for *oben* (top). It is fortunate that the stop trees inside the console and those inside the lower case are of different lengths in order to be able to tell them apart. The console tree lengths were instrumental in determining the original height of the console whose base is lost. Most of the original tree positions inside the lower case could be determined from existing upper bearings or from the relationship of the tree to the iron rockers mounted on the lower case side walls.

Wind System

The wind system of the organ consists of three large, single-fold, wedge-shaped bellows and various wooden ducts that channeled the wind to the windchests in the organ. The bellows were of course pumped when the organ was built, almost a hundred years before the advent of electricity, by manually depressing a large wooden lever beneath each bellows. This in turn lifted the top plate of the bellows and drew in air through a leather-covered valve in the bottom of the bellows. When the person acting as the pumper, known as a *calcant,* gently released pressure on the lever, the intake valve closed and stone weights on top of the bellows pushed the air trapped inside through the wind trunks and into the windbox of the windchests.

Early records seem to indicate that the organ was built to be pumped by a calcant in the church attic. This would have presented difficulties in communication and it was when the organ was scarcely two years old that a notation was recorded in the Salem Diary on October 14, 1802:

FIGURE 12. Photo showing the three large wedge-bellows in position in the attic of Home Moravian Church. The bellows were originally pumped in the church attic but were changed very early to be able to be pumped beside the organ in the gallery. These bellows may be the earliest preserved example of their kind in the United States. *Photograph courtesy of Taylor & Boody Organbuilders.*

The Singstunden were omitted this week while the bellows of the organ were being changed so that they could be blown by treading in the organ gallery.

Since the organ was out of commission for a time to accomplish this, it seems that the modification was more complicated than just dropping ropes or something similar from the ends of the pumping levers into the balcony to some sort of treading station. What exactly had been changed?

The earliest photo of the organ, from c. 1860 (with the gas lights), shows clearly two aspects of the original wind system. Three rods descend from the attic above and disappear into the right outermost tower of the organ. These must have been attached to the bellows pumping levers in the attic and to the pumping treadles that had been added to the right side of the organ. Just to the outside of the organ case at the rear wall on the left side of the organ is visible a wind duct running down the side of the organ case. Indeed, the layout of the windlines inside the case clearly shows that the wind at one time (probably from the beginning until much later) entered the organ case at the left rear corner.

The layout of the three bellows and the support rack that held them in the Home Church attic suggests that this may not be the original configuration of the bellows and rack. The main horizontal windline that exits the bellows system was not positioned above the place where the windline shown in the 1860 photo would have exited the attic floor. If the entire bellows and framework were rotated 90 degrees from where they last were in the church so that the pumping levers faced the church tower, the horizontal windline exit would coincide with the position of the vertical windline to the organ below. However, in this position, it would not be possible to drop ropes or rods through the ceiling below to pump from the balcony because these would fall inside the pedal pipes. It seems at least plausible, if not outright likely, that the bellows and frame were indeed rotated to place the pumping levers to the right side of the organ and making it possible to establish a pumping station in the balcony. This would have necessitated an additional windline to be constructed in the attic to connect the two windlines that had been separated. This would also have lengthened the overall run of the windline from the bellows to the windchests by as much as 33 percent more than the original. It is possible that in such a lightly winded organ this would have caused problems with wind stability and could possibly have led to consequent pitch and tuning problems.

A later photo of the organ, taken after the 1870 rebuilding, shows that the vertical windline outside the organ case had been removed and another photo, from around 1885, shows that the windline supplying the organ from the bellows had been moved inside the case on the right side near the pumping rods. At some time during the late nineteenth century, additional round metal windlines were fitted from this later vertical windline to each of the Hauptwerk and Hinterwerk windboxes, evidently to prevent wind starvation when all the stops, including the later additions, were drawn by providing a bit more wind to the windchests.

There is evidence in the pipework that the wind pressure of the organ was raised during the latter part of the nineteenth century. This may have been in part due to the changing fashion in organbuilding of the time and in part an attempt to rectify deficiencies in the wind system. Whatever the reason, it would appear that the increased pressure had a disastrous effect on the bellows themselves. Both end ribs of all three bellows were broken and crudely repaired. Since the bellows were last releathered in 1885, it would seem likely that the breakage of the ribs and the repairs happened after that time, otherwise the repairs would have been carried out in a more professional manner. This re-leathering was done with extremely heavy leather that was both glued and nailed in place on the ribs and side of the bellows plates. This was undoubtedly the work of a local craftsman, perhaps a harness maker.

A surprising amount of the original wind system has been preserved albeit with some reconfiguration and holes cut in windlines

FIGURE 13. Notation inside one of the bellows from the releathering in 1885:

Repaired Aug. 11th 1885 by

F. C. Meinung	W. H. Miller	
J. D. Fogle	Windy John Fogle	
	Leikes watermelons and the gals	W. F. Miller lifter

Photograph courtesy of Taylor & Boody Organbuilders.

here and there. The bellows system may be the earliest preserved version in the United States containing three single-fold wedge bellows.

The bellows had remained in place in the Home Church attic from the inauguration of the church and organ in 1800 until their removal for restoration in March of 2003. Each bellows is made with an upper and lower plate of yellow pine that has been painted with hide glue on the inside. An oak end is secured to the hinge end of each plate with wedged mortise-and-tenon joints. An oak crosspiece has been mounted at the other end of each plate by means of a long sliding dovetail. The bellows are hinged with iron hinges and the ribs of yellow pine are lined with paper on the inside. The end ribs have pages from a book of German sermons and the long ribs are covered with an English-language newspaper from Philadelphia with

FIGURE 14. Photo of the papers glued inside the end ribs of one of the bellows. These pages are part of a book of commentaries on the Old Testament from 1776 by Carl Rudolph Reichel. *Photograph courtesy of Taylor & Boody Organbuilders.*

FIGURE 15. Photo of a portion of newspaper glued to the inside of one of the side ribs of one of the bellows. The paper is an English-language newspaper from Philadelphia, *The Universal Gazette,* from December 13, 1798.

Photograph courtesy of Taylor & Boody Organbuilders.

various dates around 1798 suggesting that the bellows may have been made in Pennsylvania. From the date, it is possible that Bachmann may have also taken these parts on his trip to Salem before the rest of the organ was built. The intake and back-check valves in the bellows appear to be original, possibly with newer leather.

The windlines are all made of the heavy yellow pine found in the casework and are, for the most part remarkably intact and complete.

Windchests

Well preserved are the three large original windchests of the organ's divisions: Hauptwerk or main manual; Hinterwerk or second manual; and Pedal. Each division has a single windchest, which makes the Hauptwerk windchest with its seven stops especially massive.

The chests are of identical construction although there is a slight variation in the materials used for the Pedal windchest. They are of of typical slider windchest construction with yellow pine toeboards; walnut sliders and bearers; walnut and oak sponsels; maple, walnut, and oak ribs forming the grid with the tone channels; walnut sponsels on the bottom; walnut pallets; and a yellow pine windbox.

Sponsel construction consists of wooden pieces being inset and tightly fit and glued between the grid ribs to form the top and bottom of the channels above each of which sit the pipes for a given note on the keyboard and below which is the pallet that is attached via the playing action to the individual keys. Sponsel construction for windchests is not as common as the so-called table construction where a solid plank of wood is glued across the tops of the ribs and chest rails. Table construction is easier to make but has the disadvantage of the table cracking due to shrinkage of the wide piece of wood in the dry seasons and subsequent runs of wind from one channel to the next causing pipes to play on channels other than those intended. Sponsel windchests also crack due to winter dryness but the resulting cracks will not cause runs from one channel to another but result in wind leaks only when the key is depressed.

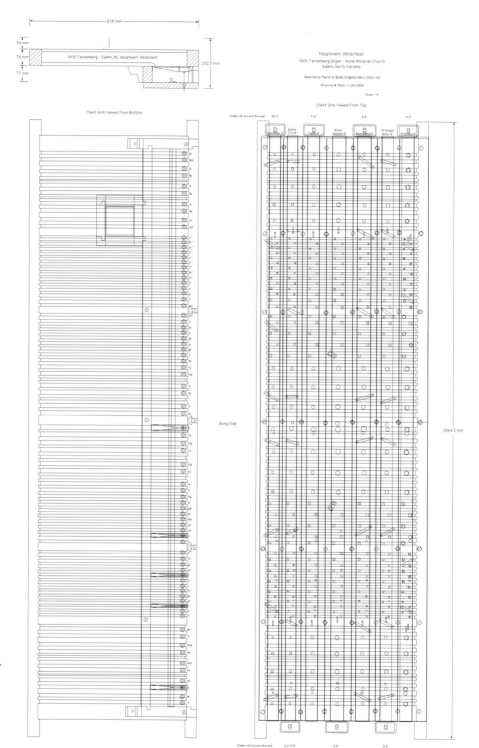

FIGURE 16. CAD drawing of the Hauptwerk windchest made during the documentation phase of the organ restoration. *Courtesy of Taylor & Boody Organbuilders.*

FIGURE 17. View of the two manual windchests in place in the lower case of the organ (viewed from the back of the organ). The toeboards have been removed exposing the sliders on the windchest tops. The four-stop Hinterwerk windchest is in the foreground and the seven-stop Hauptwerk windchest is close to the organ front separated by a narrow tuning walkboard. *Photograph courtesy of Taylor & Boody Organbuilders.*

All three windchests have developed quite a number of cracks over the years mostly from the long years of storage in the hot and cold church attic. The Hauptwerk chest survived in relatively good condition. A couple of holes about ¾″ in diameter have been drilled up into the toeboards apparently while the chest lay upside down on the attic floor. One of the holes went deep through the toeboard and slider and well down into the wind channel before the driller, who may have been hanging lights in the sanctuary below, realized that something was wrong and stopped to investigate. The rearmost toeboard originally containing the pipes of the Sub (sic) Octav 2′ (Tan-

FIGURE 18. View of windchest channels in the Hauptwerk windchest used for coupling that manual to the Pedal. The holes visible in the rib cause the two channels to communicate such that when a Pedal coupler pallet opens, the stops drawn on the Hauptwerk manual sound. *Photograph courtesy of Taylor & Boody Organbuilders.*

nenberg made the mistake of calling this stop Sub instead of Super Octav in several of his organ dispositions) was drilled to accept the treble pipes of the Quinte 3′ at some point. The two stops would have sounded together whenever the 2′ stop knob was drawn. As stated previously, this windchest also had extra pallets and channels for the Hauptwerk-to-Pedal coupler. These channels were connected to their corresponding channels for the Hauptwerk manual in such a way that if the Pedal pallet were opened by the engaged coupler, those stops that were drawn on the Hauptwerk manual would play in the Pedal.

The Hinterwerk windchest had an extension applied to its rear edge to allow the addition of two stops utilizing pipes from the 1798 Saal organ. This extension and the subsequent drilling of new holes and the plugging of some of the original holes in the chest top were the only significant changes to this windchest.

Both of the manual chests have maple rails for the long outside edges of the windchest grid. The end ribs are made of maple with the remaining ribs of oak and walnut. The Pedal windchest is made with oak rails and end ribs but is otherwise of the same construction as the manual chests.

All three windchests originally had leather pull-down wire seals, or *pulpeten.* These were replaced in 1870 with new iron pull-down wires and brass strips through which the pull-down wires passed. Portions of the original pulpeta leather strips were preserved inside the windboxes.

Tannenberg used a clever system of color-coding the channels of the windchests on their tops by using oak sponsels for the channels that were actually used for pallets and pipes and walnut sponsels for

FIGURE 19. Photo of the unrestored Hauptwerk windchest on the left and the restored Hinterwerk windchest on the right. The palletbox of the Hauptwerk windchest has been opened. Remnants of the original pulpeten leather can be seen on the inside of the palletbox bottom. *Photograph courtesy of Taylor & Boody Organbuilders.*

the unused or dead channels. This makes for a very colorful look on the windchest top with the sliders and bearers removed and would undoubtedly have been of tremendous value when laying out the pipes on the windchest grid.

The Pedal windchest is also well preserved with very little having been done to it other than the aforementioned changes to the pallet pull-downs. The original bed leather under the two sliders was in good enough condition to warrant retaining it in the restored windchest.

All three windchests originally had inset oak bung boards on the front of the windbox and these were all replaced with a single yellow pine bung board screwed to the front of the pallet box during the 1870 rebuilding.

Pipework

The most remarkable aspect of the organ's pipework is the fact that, despite the organ's long storage and numerous moves, nearly all of the original pipes still exist. Of the original 644 pipes, only seventeen are missing. It was not an easy matter to locate all the pipes.

The pipes had been sorted and placed in storage trays by North Carolina organbuilder Norman Ryan in the 1970s. When the organ was assembled for study in Old Salem's Horton Center Gallery in 1998, the pipes were once more carefully sorted and catalogued. As stated above, Paula Locklair had previously discovered an early copy of the original stoplists. Possession of this information made it possible to determine with certainty that additional sets of pipes that had been added to the Home Church organ in the 1870 rebuild were indeed pipes that had come from the 1798 Saal

FIGURE 20. Inscription from the ds′ pipe of the Principal 8′ of the Hauptwerk. This is typical of the markings on the pipes thought to be in Tannenberg's hand. Note the symbol added to the "D" designating this as a sharp pipe (ds). *Photograph courtesy of Taylor & Boody Organbuilders.*

FIGURE 21. Four of the five burlap-wrapped bundles of pipes found in the attic of the second Boys' School. These bundles contained 145 pipes, mostly from the Octave 4′, Quint 3′, and Octav 2′ stops. It is possible that these pipes were removed from the Home Church organ before the rest of the organ and stored. Perhaps there were plans to replace the pipes with pipes from different stops in an attempt to modernize the organ and thus prolong its usefulness. *Photograph courtesy of Taylor & Boody Organbuilders*

Tannenberg organ. However, once these pipes were separated from the Home Church Pipework, it was evident that a substantial number of pipes from the Principal Octav 4′, Quinte 3′, and Octav 2′ were not in storage with the rest of the organ.

Searches of all known storage areas of the organ as well as some unlikely areas such as the present Home Church organ and the organs in Bethania and Bethabara were carried out. After weeks of looking, it was suggested that all or part of the organ had been stored for a time in the attic of the Second Boys' School of Salem. There were reports that some old pipes were still stored there wrapped in burlap. A visit to the Boys' School attic confirmed that indeed a number of pipes had been sewn into five coarse burlap bundles and stuffed back into the eaves. There was no doubt that these were Tannenberg pipes from the construction and unique handwritten notations on the pipe feet. All told, these bundles yielded up some 145 pipes including a façade pipe from the Saal organ. This was a tremendous boost for the restoration effort since the few remaining missing pipes are scattered throughout the various stops and replacements could readily be made from their neighbors.

The organ originally contained 376 metal pipes and 268 wooden pipes. The ratio of wooden pipes to metal is high by today's standards. This shows clearly that Tannenberg had developed some very clear ideas as to what sorts of sounds he felt were needed and useful in an organ built for a Moravian church. Of the thirteen stops six are at 8′ pitch with one 16′ stop in the pedal and four stops at 4′pitch. This accounts for all but two of the stops in the entire organ and those two, the Quinte 3′ and the Octav 2′, are part of the organ's principal chorus useful for accompanying congregational singing.

The pipework underwent the most significant changes that the organ endured. It appears that the organ remained more or less tonally intact until the latter half of the nineteenth century. George Corrie added two swell boxes to the treble pipes on either end of the Hinterwerk windchest in the mid-nineteenth century, but there is no evidence that tonal changes were made until the 1870 rebuild.

According to the 1870 Salem Diary, the changes to the pipework were made sometime before December 24th of that year. The sorts of changes that were carried out are consistent with the direction organbuilding in general had moved during the nineteenth century. As stated before, it seems that the wind pressure of the organ was raised. This was done simply by adding more weight to the bellows tops to increase their output pressure. This may have been done in an attempt to increase the volume of the organ in general. It undoubtedly had numerous consequences. In addition to overloading the bellows to the point that the end ribs cracked, the gently voiced pipes would have been forced to overblow. To correct this, the toeholes of the pipes were closed and the cutups raised. The toeholes of

FIGURE 22. Photo of the unrestored pipes on the cs side of the Hauptwerk windchest in the organ as it was assembled in 1998. The stops are, from front (top) to back (bottom): Principal 8, Principal Octav 4´, Quintadena 8´, Gross Gedact 8´ (wood), Flauta 4´ (wood), Quinte 3´, and Sub Octav 2´. *Photograph courtesy of Taylor & Boody Organbuilders.*

the metal pipes were hammered closed—some to very small openings. The wooden pipes were restricted at the foot by inserting wedges of wood to regulate the amount of wind that could enter the pipe. If the intention of raising the wind pressure was to increase the organ's volume, the closing of the toeholes and raising of the cutups would have negated this to a great extent.

Most original principal pipes in Tannenberg's remaining instruments seem to have had their mouth openings cut open such that the height of the upper lip above the lower lip versus the mouth width is in the approximate ratio of 1:4. Some of the pipes in the Home Church organ still show this ratio while the others appear to have been raised higher, especially in the center of the pipe—a so-called "arched" cutup. Some of the wooden pipes may have undergone the same raising of their cutups but this was more difficult to do on the wooden pipes and must have been done either with a file or rasp or combination of cutting, filing, and/or rasping. The windways created between the lower lip of the pipes and the forward edge of the languid were undoubtedly altered from the original.

Numerous samples of pipe metal were analyzed to determine the lead/tin alloys used throughout the organ. Trace elements were also measured. The results of these tests are shown in the accompanying table.

TABLE 1. Semiquantitative Analyses of Tannenberg Pipe Metal, Concentrations in Weight Percentage

Date & Place of manufacture	1800 Salem, NC				
Date Tested	12/14/00 *				
Pipe	Solder— Hauptwerk P8 pipe #10	Hinterwerk Viola di Gamba 8' H	Hauptwerk Principal 8' Pipe #10	Hauptwerk Octave 4' Fs Tuning Flap	Hinterwerk Viola di Gamba 8' H
Sn (tin)	39.0000	39.0000	39.0000	39.0000	39.0000
Pb (lead)	60.1527	60.4935	60.3278	60.6239	60.6918
Sb (antimony)	0.1500	0.1000	0.4000	0.1600	0.1800
Cu (copper)	0.1900	0.2500	0.1700	0.0800	0.0700
Ag (silver)	0.0150	0.0100	0.0110	0.0700	0.0150
Bi (bismuth)	0.4500	0.1200	0.0280	0.0075	0.0048
Mg (magnesium)	0.0022	0.0008	0.0011	0.0014	0.0010
Si (silicon)	0.0160	0.0096	0.0330	0.0290	0.0160
Fe (iron)	0.0020	*0.0010*	0.0036	0.0059	0.0034
Ni (nickle)	0.0022	0.0010	0.0023	0.0021	0.0020
Co (cobalt)	*0.0006*	*0.0006*	*0.0006*	*0.0006*	*0.0006*
Al (aluminum)	0.0011	*0.0002*	0.0016	0.0026	0.0009
Ca (calcium)	0.0072	0.0022	0.0100	0.0060	0.0035
Cd (cadmium)	*0.0060*	*0.0060*	*0.0060*	*0.0060*	*0.0060*
In (indium)	*0.0050*	*0.0060*	*0.0050*	*0.0050*	*0.0050*
As (arsenic)	–	–	–	–	–
Totals	100.0000	100.0009	100.0000	100.0000	100.0000

(table continues)

*These samples were too small for chemical tin text.

Numers in **bold italics** were below the threshold of the test indicated; numbers in *plain italics* are traces present less than indicated amount.

(table 1 continued)

Pipe	1800 Salem, NC — 2/6/02*					1774 Trinity Lanc. Pa — 11/12/02	1802 Madison, VA	— 12/14/00
	Hauptwerk Octave 4' fs" top	Hinterwerk Viola di Gamba 8' e'	Hauptwerk P8' fs Languid	Hauptwerk P8' solder— var. pipes	Hauptwerk Principal 8' d' (façade)	Oberwerk P8' Façade pipe (dumb)	Flöte 4' c''' Broken from tuning flap	Principal 4' façade pipe overlengh
Sn (tin)	39.9300	37.2500	26.1000	57.7000	65.9000	48.8000	32.8000	39.0000
Pb (lead)	59.4137	62.4263	73.5657	40.1821	33.4621	50.3113	66.5131	60.1432
Sb (antimony)	0.3200	0.1800	0.2300	0.1100	0.3600	0.4400	0.3600	0.3800
Cu (copper)	0.1600	0.0039	0.0004	0.2700	0.1400	0.2500	0.1700	0.3400
Ag (silver)	0.0068	0.0047	0.0054	0.0064	0.0041	0.0064	0.0076	0.0110
Bi (bismuth)	0.0170	0.0039	0.0028	1.6000	0.0150	0.0720	0.0220	0.0400
Mg (magnesium)	0.0071	0.0140	0.0065	0.0099	0.0020	0.0029	0.0033	0.0008
Si (silicon)	0.0630	0.0350	0.0150	0.0370	0.0150	0.0130	0.0170	0.0520
Fe (iron)	0.0011	0.0015	0.0010	0.0013	0.0008	0.0006	0.0013	0.0095
Ni (nickle)	0.0027	0.0020	*0.0010*	0.0031	0.0022	0.0019	0.0027	0.0017
Co (cobalt)	***0.0009***	***0.0009***	***0.0009***	***0.0009***	***0.0010***	***0.0010***	***0.0010***	0.0030
Al (aluminum)	0.0140	0.0120	0.0067	0.0130	*0.0010*	*0.0010*	0.0010	0.0008
Ca (calcium)	0.0027	0.0048	0.0036	0.0053	0.0018	0.0049	0.0060	0.0070
Cd (cadmium)	***0.0080***	***0.0030***	***0.0080***	***0.0080***	***0.0100***	***0.0100***	***0.0100***	***0.0060***
In (indium)	***0.0030***	***0.0500***	***0.0030***	***0.0030***	***0.0050***	***0.0050***	***0.0050***	***0.0050***
As (arsenic)	***0.0500***	***0.0080***	***0.0500***	***0.0500***	***0.0800***	***0.0800***	***0.0800***	–
Totals	100.0000	100.0000	100.0000	100.0000	100.0000	100.0000	100.0000	100.0000

*These are larger (½ gram) samples.

Numers in **bold italics** were below the threshold of the test indicated; numbers in *plain italics* are traces present less than indicated amount.
From Spectrodyne Consultants, Simi Valley, California.

The metal pipes are fairly typical in their construction with the exception of the languids. The metal for the bodies and feet has been scraped or planed smooth on both sides, perhaps, in part, to regulate the metal thickness. Most bodies are significantly thinner at their tops than at the mouth ends. The mouths have lines scored lightly on the inside of the pipe and are then pressed in. The façade mouths have scored and pressed round or Roman lips. The upper and lower lips of the pipes are aligned more or less directly over each other. The leading edges of both lips are skived almost to a point on the outside of the pipe. The toes of the pipes are coned only slightly and they are fit snuggly into a counterbored hole in the toeboards.

Tannenberg's metal pipes have a unique languid form. The main bevel on the top at the front of the languid is quite shallow—around 25 degrees on average. The languid was cast on a surface that allowed the front edge to be formed much thicker than the rest of the languid. There are signs on the bottom of the larger languids of cloth that lined the surface upon which the languid was cast. The main bevel at the languid front extends from about the midpoint, thickness-wise of the languid front. A large counter-bevel extends downward from the upper bevel and is angled slightly toward the rear of the pipe—about 5 degrees. The juncture of the main and counter-bevels is approximately the midpoint of the languid thickness at the front and this point was assembled onto the foot of the pipe so that it is basically even with the top of the lower lip. The lower lip is curved outward from the windway such that the windways were ever so slightly larger at the top than at the lower edge of the languid.

FIGURE 23. Damage to the languid face of a large metal pipe. The smaller nicks in the face appear to have been put there by Tannenberg prior to the assembly of the pipe. The larger gashes and punctures are from later revoicing attempts. The large counterface or counterbevel is original. *Photograph courtesy of Taylor & Boody Organbuilders.*

With this sort of construction, the alignment of the various parts of the pipes is critical to the speech of the pipe. Normal voicing techniques such as tapping the forward edge of the languid up or down to effect the pipe speech by redirecting the windsheet are largely ineffective. The degree to which the windway leads the wind into or out of the pipe has the greatest effect on the pipe's speed of speech. The position of the upper lip of the pipe relative to the windway can be changed slightly by bending it inward or outward but the effect this has on the speech of the pipe is slight.

Judging from the extant organs, Tannenberg seems to have pre-nicked the larger metal pipes by making small angled cuts in the counter-bevel on the languids before the pipes were assembled. The nicks that appear to be original could not be put into the languid's leading edge after the pipe was assembled because this surface would be so far below the upper edge of the lower lip. This languid construction mimics to a great extent the effect of the construction of wooden pipes on their voicing.

Additional nicking was added during the nineteenth century revoicing. These nicks were ill conceived and show a lack of understanding of Tannenberg's languid construction. Most were put into the upper bevel and extended into the windway and also into the inside edge of the lower lip. These nicks did not for the most part penetrate to the bottom of the counter-bevel. As such, they were limited in their effect on the pipe speech and probably succeeded in only muffling somewhat the onset of the pipe speech and causing an indistinct quality to the ongoing tone.

The organ's principal pipes (Principal 8′, Octave 4′, Quinte 3′, and Octav 2′) are all very nearly the same scale. The Principal 8′ pipes inside the organ have an "8" written below the note name on the upper body. The Octav 4′ pipes have their note names underlined on the side of the foot. The Quint 3′ and Octave 2′ however, have no differentiating markings. Aside from a few pipes in the bass of the Quint, which are marked with a "q", it is nearly impossible to tell these stops apart.

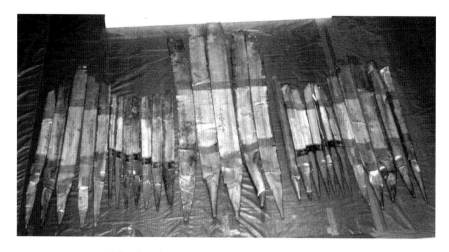

FIGURE 24. The façade pipes as they appeared during the organ assembly at Old Salem in 1998. The pipes are laid out on the floor in the order they would stand in the organ. All of the pipes are sounding pipes and were able to be restored. *Photograph courtesy of Taylor & Boody Organbuilders.*

For that matter, all the pipes in the organ are minimally marked. This would not have presented as much of a problem for the restorers had the metal pipes from the Saal organ not been mixed into the organ. There is reasonable certainty that the pipes of the Quintadena 8´, Viola di Gambe 8´, and Octave 4´ for each organ have been correctly identified.

It is quite interesting to note that all the D pipes in the organ sport the same capital "D" as in Tannenberg's first name. Other pipes in the organ have capital letters for the note names in the bass registers and lower case letters in the treble. The capital D on all of those pipes seems to be a kind of signature on the part of Tannenberg.

The pitch of the organ was changed so that it eventually ended up at the modern pitch of a´ = 440 Hz. This was done in part by moving the pipes up ½ step in their respective stops so that what was low C became the new Cs and so on. This meant that the upper pipe in each stop was no longer needed and indeed a number of the stops of the organ are now missing their uppermost pipe or a nearby neighbor. Pipes of some sort must have been inserted into the now empty low C holes, although these pipes have not been identified. Exceptions were made with the Pedal pipes in that they were not moved but merely cut off to the new pitch. The façade pipes were likewise not moved but cut away in the back to arrive at the new pitch. In this case a new low C pipe was not needed but a pipe was inserted into the stop near the point where the pipes go from the façade to inside the case standing on the windchest.

The façade pipes were painted and stenciled in Victorian style in the late nineteenth century. This had the unexpected good fortune of protecting to some extent the original surface of the façade pipes during the long storage of the organ.

The pipes suffered a great deal of damage during the storage period of the organ. For the first 60 years or so, the pipes were merely

FIGURE 25. Damage to the façade pipes. This pipe was nearly torn in two pieces at the body and foot seam. The seam was separated and the body and foot rounded up separately and then re-soldered. Note the beautifully preserved surface of the more than 200-year old metal. *Photograph courtesy of Taylor & Boody Organbuilders.*

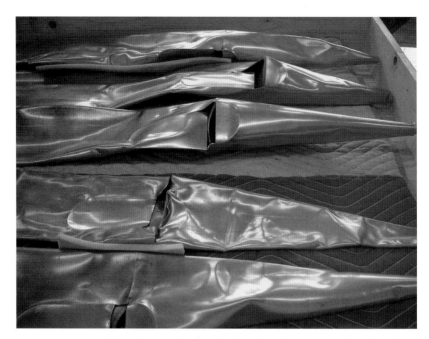

FIGURE 25A. Typical condition of the façade pipes after the late-nineteenth-century paint was stripped from them. The surface of the metal is remarkably well preserved in spite of the dents and flattening. The paint protected the original surface of the pipes from many scratches that they would otherwise have received. All of these pipes were restored to playing condition. *Photograph courtesy of Taylor & Boody Organbuilders.*

stacked up on the floor of the church attic or wherever they may have been stored. Metal pipes are not designed to withstand the forces placed upon them when they not standing upright. Stacking them up will invariably cause them to deform and collapse. There are stories that the façade pipes, which emerged from storage basically flattened, were walked upon by children playing in the church or school attic. Others even crushed some of the smaller wooden pipes during storage.

It is surprising and in many respects a miracle that the organ has survived into the twenty-first century. We would be much the poorer without it. It is fortunate that a number of people over the years have actively taken part in the preservation of the organ. The actual restoration is the result of careful thinking and planning over quite a number of years long before any actual work began on the organ itself.

Guidelines were developed at the Taylor & Boody workshop to be observed during the restoration process. These may be summarized as follows:

1. Adequate preparation before any work is begun.

2. Maintaining respect for the original character of the organ.

3. Consideration of reversibility of restoration techniques.

4. Minimizing additional interventions into the organ.

5. Careful recording of restoration work carried out.

Due to the fact that the major changes and additions to the organ were from the 1870 rebuild and that this had involved the use of pipes from the 1798 Saal Tannenberg, it seemed a reasonable goal to restore the organ primarily to its 1800 condition. This would free up the metal pipes for the Saal organ for its eventual restoration and would remove alterations of questionable integrity and reliability. The few parts that would need to be removed could be preserved as historical artifacts in themselves. This would include the 1845 swell boxes and their control mechanism and the additions to the Hinterwerk windchest.

All existing conditions were documented and pho-

FIGURE 26. The restored case and façade. Details of impost and cornice moldings can clearly be seen. The restored and re-gilded pipe shades cover the tops of the original façade pipes. *Photograph courtesy of Taylor & Boody Organbuilders.*

tographed before any work was performed. Digital photography matured at a particularly advantageous time for this project with over 5000 photographs being taken relating to the research for the project and photo documentation of the work actually performed.

The Organ Case

The first step in the restoration of the organ case began with the trial assembly of the entire organ in the Old Salem's Horton Center Gallery in 1998. Armed with information about the condition and completeness of the organ case, the organ was moved to the Taylor & Boody workshop in Staunton, Virginia, in 1999.

Frank Welsh, of Welsh Color & Conservation, Inc., who prepared thorough paint documentation, took paint samples from various points on the case. A primary concern was that the original coats of paint contained lead oxide as a white pigment. Subsequent layers were flaking off and chipping to the extent that the original layers were exposed where white dust containing this lead oxide could be rubbed off.

Various tactics for dealing with the paint were discussed. It was suggested that we could simply paint the organ once again. This would preserve all the layers of paint but did not solve the flaking and chipping problem, which could be expected to continue. It would also be difficult to prepare the surface evenly for another paint layer without abrading the previous layer which would stir up the lead contamination. The moldings on the cornices had suffered especially from the many layers already on the case and the dentils and meanders were becoming quite indistinct with thick paint buildup.

It was decided to strip the case to bare wood and to begin again with only the layers of paint to be applied by the restorers. A four-inch wide witness strip remains intact on the left side of the case from top to bottom just in front of the access door. This preserves examples of all the paint that had been on the case for future reference while allowing the rest of the case to return to a look as close as

possible to its original. Many different chemical strippers of widely varying strengths were tested and all proved unsatisfactory. A lye-based powder soluble in water was tried and showed good results in removing even the oldest layers of casein paint. It had the added advantage of keeping the lead oxide bound up in paste form so that respiration of the pigments would not be a significant problem for those involved in the stripping operation.

Repairs to the woodwork per se were more straightforward. Each problem was carefully evaluated and possible solutions studied before any action was taken. Cuts in the lower panels on the right side of the organ were filled in. Holes that had been crudely cut into the cornice moldings on the right side of the organ for the balcony pumping station were filled. The two missing front stiles were remade using historic photos for reference. Wood for the reproduction parts came from salvaged yellow pine beams. The reclaimed wood closely matches the original material.

A floor frame was constructed to place beneath the organ to help register the parts, and especially to provide accurate points for referencing the stop action trees and other action parts. There is good

FIGURE 28. Console during restoration. Because the console was originally installed against the balcony railing, it had no back and the end panels were omitted. It was necessary to construct these parts to harmonize visually and to agree physically with the lower case and base of the organ. *Photograph courtesy of Taylor & Boody Organbuilders.*

reason to believe that the organ originally had a floor frame and that it was lost or discarded at the time of the organ's removal from Home Church.

Similarly, the organ case had originally been coped and fastened to the wall of the church behind it. It would not be possible to do this when re-erecting the case in the new Old Salem Visitor Center. To maintain the structural integrity that attachment to the wall had afforded the case, it was decided to build a rudimentary backframe for the case just behind the Pedal windchest.

The main portion of the case housing the manual chests and pipes had originally been separated from the pedal chest and pipes behind by a frame with removable panels. This had apparently been discarded when the swell boxes were added to the Hinterwerk. The missing frame pieces and panels were reconstructed using old wood. The panels were made of white pine instead of the heavier yellow pine to make them easier to handle and less likely to be dropped during future servicing of the organ.

The base of the console had never had a back or end panels due to its original integral construction with the balcony railing. It was decided to reconstruct end panels and a back for the console as they could have been in a Tannenberg organ where the console was entirely freestanding. Unfortunately there are only two extant examples to consult and the 1787 Lititz console had itself been largely reconstructed. The Saal organ console provided valuable ideas for the base and panels but in the end, the existing parts and old photos of the Home Church organ gave the best indications of how to proceed. The reconstructed parts were the result of painstaking study and many hours of trial and error.

The floorboards under the bench and pedalboard were probably integral with the balcony floor when the organ was installed in the church. A section of this balcony floor level was reconstructed fitting it between the extant sections of base molding on the main case and the sides of the console.

Repairs were made to the pipe shade carvings using the historical photos and the mirror mate to the shades on the other side of the organ as references. Paint tests on the shades showed that they were originally coated with a ground gesso base and gold leafed. They had been painted over with a bronze paint.

Surviving sections of the gallery fretwork that originally topped the impost were used to recreate the missing portions. The carvings and the fretwork were sent to Sandy Jensen of Hanover, Virginia, who carried out the professional restoration of the surface and regilding.

It is questionable whether the small access door in the lower section of the right side of the upper case is original. Its use for tuning access into the organ is limited, but it was decided to retain it rather than to fill it in with a panel.

The rear access doors to the lower case had been substantially altered over the years but one set of original iron hinges remained. A matching set was hand-forged by the workshop of Peter Ross in Williamsburg, Virginia. Ross's shop also supplied hand forged nails for various parts of the case.

Playing Action

The playing action of the organ was in remarkably good condition. The rollerboards, square rails, and bundles of trackers and a number of original tracker guides all were in good condition. Little had been altered over the years.

FIGURE 29. The restored keyboards for the organ. The keys are entirely new with levers of walnut, natural tops of ebony, and sharps of stained walnut with legal ivory tops. Dimensions were determined by studying the 1802 keyboard in the Tannenberg organ at Hebron Lutheran Church in Madison, Virginia. Other clues came from study of the original keyframes which were reused. *Photograph courtesy of Taylor & Boody Organbuilders.*

New keyboards were made using the 1802 Tannenberg organ at Madison, Virginia, as a model. The original key frames had been reused for the 1870 rebuilding when new balance and front guide pins had been installed. The old pin holes were clearly evident and it was a simple matter to return to the original key lengths and balance points. The octave spacing had been widened and the key fronts lengthened when the keys were replaced in 1870. These were reduced to the same measurements from the Madison keyboard, which corresponds well to the old keyframe pin holes.

The reconstructed keys used walnut levers with ebony natural tops and walnut sharps stained black and capped with ivory. The keys were not sanded but were hand planed to their final surface finish. A key front nosing was applied using the Madison model and decorative lines were cut at the rear edge of the natural tops in front of the sharps.

The preserved parts of the old Hinterwerk to Hauptwerk manual coupler were re-used in a new coupler that was worked out conjecturally from those old parts. The new coupler works well and likely behaves much like the lost original.

The square rails required only some straightening of the brass squares and a thorough cleaning again to be ready for use. The rollerboards needed a few new roller arms and pivot studs to be made. These were installed and the rollers and boards were cleaned. Wear on the arms and roller bearings appeared to be minimal and this was deemed to be within an acceptable range for the restored organ. No felt bushings were used to help silence action parts.

FIGURE 30. View of the restored playing action squares of the Hauptwerk and Pedal coupler. Both the wooden and the brass squares are original while the trackers and wire ends are reproductions. *Photograph courtesy of Taylor & Boody Organbuilders.*

Due to the complexity of the sorting of the old trackers and the fragility of the iron wire tracker ends, it was decided to make a new set of trackers for the organ. Tannenberg's son-in-law, Bachmann may not have taken the time to carefully cut the trackers as precisely to length as he could have. There were indications that the rollers and squares were not set up at "half-motion" where the rollers and squares move equal amounts above and below their mid-positions. The playability of the organ may have suffered as a result. New trackers allowed the restorers the chance to balance the action with

FIGURE 31. View inside the organ of the restored rollerboard and playing action under the Hauptwerk windchest. This rollerboard has rollers for each of the manual keys and pallets as well as an additional set for the pedal keys and pallets used in the Hauptwerk-to-Pedal coupler. *Photograph courtesy of Taylor & Boody Organbuilders.*

care and deliberation to help the organ play as nicely as most of the other extant Tannenberg organs.

Tannenberg preferred to use heavy brass wire for the pallet springs in the windchests. These springs directly hold the pallets closed against the wind and provide for the return of the depressed manual keys. Using the Madison organ again as a model, the springs were made and adjusted to give the action the characteristic feel of a typical Tannenberg keyboard. The keys feel a bit heavy to our modern sensitivities, but the action works well and should give an accurate impression of playing a late-eighteenth-century American organ.

Stop Action

Many parts of the stop action had been changed to a greater or lesser extent over the years but a surprising number of original parts were found to exist. The oak stop trees with their iron end pins and forged iron arms were all extant although some of the arms had been moved or reversed. The wooden upper bearings for the stop trees in the console were preserved and provided guidance in the placement of the trees within the console. The trees were fitted into new lower bearings that were an integral part of the new floor frame system.

Some of the original upper stop tree bearings were preserved for the trees housed within the lower case but others were missing. It was possible to make an educated guess as to where the trees had stood originally based upon the iron rocker positions in the lower case. The planned positions for the trees were carefully laid out in the organ and on a computer-drawn floor plan of the entire organ to make certain that everything would function together as it might have originally without undue conflicts for space. New upper and lower bearings were constructed as needed and the trees installed in the lower case.

Many of the original walnut connecting traces were preserved and most were able to be put back into the restored organ in their original positions. Due to the moving and rearranging of some of the stops in the 1870 rebuild of the organ, some of the traces had been substantially altered or lost and replacements had to be made.

The original stop knobs on the console and their labels were missing and no traces of them have been found at this point. Unfortunately no original Tannenberg stop knobs exist on any of the extant detached consoles. The stop knobs on the Madison organ are original but the labels have been replaced. It was decided to use the Madison organ's stop knobs as a reference and to design and make new knobs in that general style but somewhat smaller to allow for the double row of stop knobs and the closer spacing of the stop rods on the Home Church organ. Parchment labels were hand lettered and placed in a recess at the front of the knobs.

Wind System

As stated previously, a large portion of the original wind system of the organ was preserved intact. The yellow pine windlines inside the case are all preserved and needed only some minor repairs to be put back into use.

The old bellows frame was left in the Home Church attic to mark the spot where the bellows once stood. There are sufficient questions surrounding the original position of the bellows in the attic and as to which parts are or are not original that it was decided to build a new frame in the same style that would be able to be freestanding in the room behind the restored organ in the Old Salem Visitor Cen-

FIGURE 32. One of the three bellows following re-leathering. The yellow pine tops and bottoms of the bellows are so heavy that the bellows produces a wind pressure of about 40mm without any additional weight on top. Special vegetable-tanned leather was used for the restoration. *Photograph courtesy of Taylor & Boody Organbuilders.*

ter. The bellows are mounted in the reconstructed frame as they likely were originally and can still be pumped manually with the original pumping levers.

In the interests of having an interactive exhibit of the organ, it was not possible to place the bellows in a space above the organ as they were in Home Church. The total length of the windline from the bellows to the organ is a bit shorter than it likely was in the organ originally but the wind characteristics are good and the organ behaves with the pumped wind very much as it likely would have originally.

A modern electric blower has been added to the wind system to allow for the possibility of organists practicing on the organ without engaging the services of a calcant. The addition of the blower was carried out in such a way that it could be removed at any point to return the organ to its pristine winding system. The blower can be turned off and the organ manually pumped without engaging or disengaging any additional apparatus.

A pile of stones was found near the bellows in the church attic.

These stones were used as weights for the top of the bellows to provide the wind pressure that had been set to support a water column in a manometer of 44mm. The pipes work well at this pressure and there is convincing evidence in the other extant Tannenberg organs to suggest that this was a normal wind pressure for David Tannenberg's organs.

Windchests

The windchests required a great deal of effort to restore them in such a way that they would provide trouble-free service in the years to come while remaining true to their original construction. Most problematic in that regard was dealing with the many cracked and leaking sponsels in the wind channels. The Pedal windchest was preserved, in most respects, in the best condition of the three before the restoration. Consequently it was decided to restore it first to explore and develop techniques that could be used later in the more complex restoration of the manual windchests.

One might reasonably ask why the cracks in the sponsels could

FIGURE 33. View of a restored pallet and pull-down wire and pulpeta seal inside the Pedal windchest. The pallet has not yet been glued in place and the brass compass spring which holds the pallet closed is not installed. *Photograph courtesy of Taylor & Boody Organbuilders.*

not be simply glued back in place or filled with extra wood. This indeed would be possible but the seasonal expansion and contraction of the wood in the windchests has over two centuries established its own sort of control joints and to fill them up with new wood would undoubtedly cause new cracks to form elsewhere. It was decided that it would be preferable to allow the long-established cracks to continue to move seasonally and to seal them in another way.

The chests were disassembled down to their basic grids. Due to their wedged mortise and tenon rib construction, further disassembly was neither necessary nor feasible. In the case of the Pedal windchest, the leaking sponsel cracks were sealed from the outside with strips of parchment glued over the cracks with animal hide glue. This sealed the leaking channels while preserving the integrity of the original construction and allowed for easy removal or replacement as necessary in the future. The leather beneath the sliders on the Pedal windchest was deemed usable and was preserved. It is likely that this leather is the original material from more than 200 years ago! The leather was of remarkably high quality and has been preserved to a great extent because it was sandwiched tightly between the slider and the chest and not subjected to light or direct contact with the atmosphere. The seams where different strips were joined end to end have been carefully fit together and their edges neatly skived. The edges of the holes into the channels below have been cauterized with a hot iron to keep the edges of the leather at the holes from catching on the slider holes as the sliders were moved.

In the case of the manual windchests, the cracks were repaired by cutting away a small amount of the wood of the windchest rib along the crack to a depth of about five millimeters. Into this crack was fit a new piece of wood with a piece of leather along one edge and along its bottom. These parts were glued into the routed slot with hide glue in such a way that the leather on the side of the piece of wood was glued only to the rib and not to the new filler piece. The leather will be able to absorb a great deal of the seasonal expansion and contraction of the wood along the joint. Should the wood move

FIGURE 34. Burning the pipe channel holes through the replacement bed leather beneath the sliders on the restored Hauptwerk windchest. The original leather was similarly burned to cauterize the edges of the holes. This helps to keep the leather around the holes from catching on the slider holes as the slider is moved when a stop knob is pulled on or pushed off. *Photograph courtesy of Taylor & Boody Organbuilders.*

enough to pull the leather away from the filler piece on the side, the leather along the bottom edge will continue to seal the channel and prevent a leak. Since the leather is exposed to the air only along one edge, it should remain a viable seal for some time to come.

Several broken slider drive ends were repaired and extraneous holes in the windchests and sliders were plugged. The manual windchest grids were carefully flattened and the pallet boxes reinstalled. The pallets were re-leathered with vegetable-tanned leather (which was used exclusively throughout the restoration) and glued back into the windchests. New leather pull-down seals were fabricated using the original seals on the Madison organ as a model and new

FIGURE 35. Repair process for a typical crack in the windchest sponsels (clockwise). The first photograph shows the color-coded windchest grid with the lighter oak sponsels denoting the active channels and the walnut ribs between with walnut sponsels in the unused or dead channels. *Photograph courtesy of Taylor & Boody Organbuilders.*

FIGURE 35A. The windchest sponsel repairs carried out with a walnut filler strip and leather gasket. *Photograph courtesy of Taylor & Boody Organbuilders.*

FIGURE 35B. The completed windchest sponsel repair with its expansion possibilities. *Photograph courtesy of Taylor & Boody Organbuilders.*

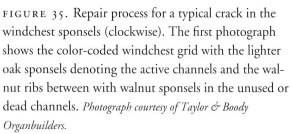

pull-down wires were made from brass wire and birch dowels. Reproduction pallet springs were made from spring-tempered brass wire and set to reflect the spring tensions from the Madison organ.

The addition to the grid of the Hinterwerk windchest was carefully removed and preserved and the extra holes in the grid and chest rail plugged with side-grained maple plugs. New walnut bearers were installed where the originals were missing and the bed leather under the sliders was replaced with similar new material on both manual windchests. The sliders were carefully shimmed to provide the proper amount of sealing while still allowing the sliders to move freely.

The various toeboards were repaired where necessary. New toeboards were made to replace the missing façade toeboards. All of the original lead tubing running from the windchest toeboards to the façade toeboards was located and repaired and re-used. New walnut rack pins were made to replace the few that were missing. Many of the rackboards had been altered substantially over the years and quite a few were broken and had missing sections. These were repaired as needed. A thin poplar board was glued under each rackboard to strengthen the original and provide support for the pipes where the rack holes had been enlarged. These additions to the bottom of the rack are done in such a way that they can be removed while preserving the original material.

FIGURE 36. The addition made to the Hinterwerk windchest channels during the 1870 rebuild. The channel addition is being separated from the original windchest rail by carefully wedging the pieces apart. The channel addition was poorly glued to the chest rail and likely caused serious leaks and runs in the windchest. *Photograph courtesy of Taylor & Boody Organbuilders.*

They do not interfere with the original rack support and pin structures in any way. These repairs are virtually invisible inside the organ.

The restored windchests were tested under wind pressure before reinstallation in the organ to prove that they were functioning as required in every respect and that all leaks have been sealed. No runs (leaks from one channel to another) nor ciphers (pipes playing without opening their respective pallets) were discovered.

Pipework

A considerable amount of the total time spent restoring the organ was required for restoring the pipes. This included a thorough documentation of the wooden and metal pipes. Diameters, wall thicknesses, lengths of bodies and feet, mouth widths and cutups, and pipe inscriptions were among the many items documented on each of the organ's pipes.

Metal pipes were washed thoroughly and their bodies and feet were made round once more. Rudimentary repairs were also carried out often including seam repairs. When the façade pipes were restored after an exceptional amount of careful planning and repair work, it was possible to determine the original pitch of the organ. Remnants of the original tuning tabs on the backs of the pipes were preserved in many of the pipes and these indicated that the organ was originally pitched a bit more than ½ step lower than modern pitch of a′ = 440 Hz at approximately 413 Hz. From the other extant Tannenberg organs and the written instructions he sent to Salem for tuning the organ, it is clear that Tannenberg was an early proponent of equal temperament. This made it possible to ascertain the pitches of the individual façade pipes and to calculate the amount necessary to be added to the remaining metal pipes in the organ to bring it back to its original pitch and tuning.

The pipes were re-racked on the toeboards using the old rackboards and supports. Where the original rackboards had been enlarged considerably during the rescaling of the organ in the late nineteenth century, a new piece of wood was added to the bottom of the original rack with hide glue so it could be removed if necessary. New holes were drilled for the pipes and the rack hole enlarged by burning with a hot, tapered iron so the pipes fit as well as possible in the rack.

The 2′ c pipe in the Principal Octav 4′ stop has an inscription on its top unique in this organ. The pipe appears to be made of a higher tin content than the rest of the stop due to its brighter appearance and therefore somewhat stronger and resistant to crushing. The inscription seems to read "gestimmt nach der Lititze Orgel" (tuned from the Lititz organ). It may be that this pipe was made strong enough to travel unscathed from Lititz to Salem and that it was to be used as the tuning reference pipe (rather than using a tuning fork) having been voiced and tuned by Tannenberg himself.

The wooden pipes were also cleaned and basic repairs carried out to make them play. This consisted mostly of flattening the back side of their caps and re-gluing them. Many of these had cupped and come loose from the front of the pipe which prevented them from playing. Some pipes needed seam repairs and to have other minor details looked after. By far the greatest portion of the work involved the lengthening of these pipes. Like their metal counterparts, they had been shortened by about one whole tone from their original pitch when the pipes were moved up ½ step and the organ was retuned. The stoppers of the Gedact 8′ and Subbass 16′ stops were re-leathered and refitted to the pipes. Existing metal tuning flaps were reused where possible on the open wooden pipes and replacements made for the others.

The pipes and sounds from the other extant Tannenberg organs were carefully studied. Similarities between the various organs as well as the obvious progress that Tannenberg made throughout his career were likewise observed and duly noted. Problems with certain aspects of the pipes required careful attention and consideration. Most problematic were changes that had been made to the languids and cutups of the pipes.

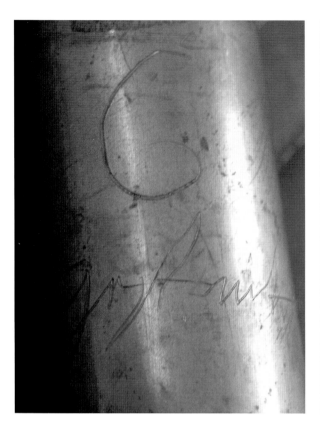 

FIGURE 37. *(left)* This image and the next two piece together the inscription on the top of the body of the tenor c (2′) pipe of the Octav 4′. There is a notation marking it as a c pipe under which it appears to read: "Gestimt nach der Litizer Orgel" (tuned from the Lititz organ). This pipe seems to be made from a higher tin content than the remainder of the stop. It could be that this was a tuning reference pipe, tuned by Tannenberg to the organ he built for his church in Lititz. The higher tin content would help insure that the carefully voiced and tuned pipe could make the arduous trip to Salem and arrive in usable condition. *Photograph courtesy of Taylor & Boody Organbuilders.*

FIGURE 37A. *(right)* Second partial inscription on the top of the body of the tenor c (2′) pipe of the Octav 4′. *Photograph courtesy of Taylor & Boody Organbuilders.*

Where cutups were clearly altered, the most seriously altered pipes were repaired first in an effort to keep as many of the pipes with their original soldering and geometric alignments as possible. Some of the pipes needed to be cut apart at the foot/body seam to repair badly damaged languids or excessively high cutups. Every effort was made to preserve the alignment of the body and the position of the upper lip above the windway and lower lip.

Due to Tannenberg's unique languid construction as previously described, the voicing possibilities of the pipes are quite limited. The usual technique of tapping the front edge of the languid slightly up or down to adjust the pipe's speech is ineffective with the large counterbevel on the languid front that protrudes down into the foot of the pipe. The position of the upper lip in and out of the pipe can be changed slightly and is useful as a fine adjustment of the pipe speech. The uppermost edge of the lower lip can be slightly bent more or less into the windway. This has the effect of speeding up the pipe speech when pressed in and slowing it down when pulled out. The parameters within which the pipes speak without overblowing or being excessively slow are quite narrow. For this reason, it seems reasonable that the sound being produced by the pipes after the restoration is very close to the sound they produced originally since most of them will not play outside these narrow boundaries. It is true that the exact volume of the pipes may vary slightly and the speed of the speech is also a subjective judgment on the part of the voicer. The tone color may have been altered by the nicking that could not be removed. The cutups

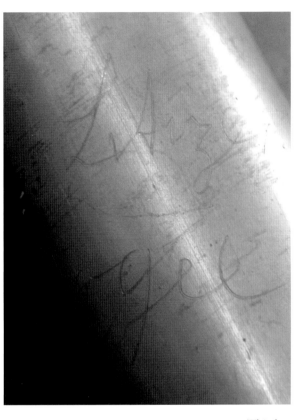

FIGURE 37B. Third partial inscription on the top of the body of the tenor c (2′) pipe of the Octav 4′. *Photograph courtesy of Taylor & Boody Organbuilders.*

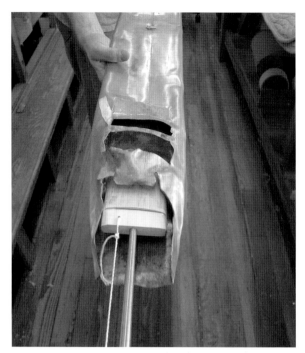

FIGURE 38. Method used for opening the bodies of crushed metal pipes. The blunt wooden wedge was carefully pushed down the inside of the pipe spreading the metal open again. Once opened, the pipe can be rounded further by placing it on successively larger diameter mandrels and tapping it on the outside with a soft beating stick. *Photograph courtesy of Taylor & Boody Organbuilders.*

of the organ pipes have been restored as carefully as possible but not in any whole-sale manner. There are undoubtedly variations from the original. It was decided that exact restoration of the cutups and languid fronts was not possible and furthermore that attempts to do so would harm the pipes irreparably. Nevertheless, the sound of the restored organ is quite compelling and seems to give an adequate impression of the organ over two centuries after its construction.

CONCLUSION

The restored Home Church Tannenberg organ is an immensely important link in the history of the organ in America between the late-eighteenth and early-nineteenth centuries. Once again in playing condition, it offers us a valid glimpse into the musical life of the young new country and specifically of the Moravian tradition at the fringes of early American settlement. The organ is also important as a remnant of the "Leiblichkeit" school of organbuilding that was once prevalent in eastern Germany. This style of organbuilding is characterized by the use of low wind pressures and consequently gentle voicing as well as an early proliferation of unison stops of pipes in the dispositions. This early-eighteenth-century style was largely eclipsed by the work of Gottfried Silbermann in the mid-eighteenth century. Virtually all of these "Leiblichkeit" organs have disappeared or have been thoroughly altered. The Home Church Tannenberg organ is the largest surviving example of this school of organbuilding in America and is among the few extant examples remaining anywhere. Tannenberg's mastery of the craft, his attention to detail, and love of his work are obvious throughout this and his other remaining instruments.

It is hoped that this organ will provide inspiration to all who see, hear, and play it. May its voice once again ring out and speak to us of the subtle, simple pleasures of life from a man who took great pride in his work and the instruments he created.

I am indeed certain that if everything is done according to the plan, the result will be one of the finest instruments I have made or designed. I myself should be glad to be present for the completion of the Organ.

I remain with warm greetings, your humble Brother,

David Tannenberg

(from a letter to Mr. Samuel Stotz, Salem 11 June 1800)

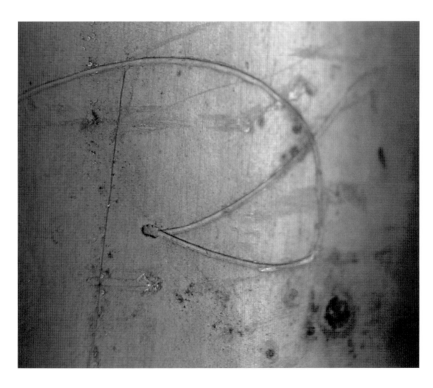

FIGURE 39. Inscription on a typical D pipe made by Tannenberg. This inscribed "D" closely resembles the initial letter in Tannenberg's signature and may have been his way of signing the pipes. While other pipes have upper case letters in the bass and lower case letters in the treble, the D pipes all have capital letters. *Photograph courtesy of Taylor & Boody Organbuilders.*

Bruce Shull is head voicer for Taylor & Boody Organbuilders in Staunton, Virginia, and headed the restoration team for the Home Moravian Church Tannenberg organ.

APPENDIX I: HOME CHURCH TANNENBERG ORGAN RESTORATION CHRONOLOGY

1910   Organ is removed from Home Church and put into storage.

1960s   Home Church asks Old Salem to store the organ to protect it from further damage.

1989   Old Salem Curator Paula Locklair has Barbara Owen—a renowned organ historian—come to assess the 1798 Tannenberg organ in the Single Brothers' House Saal and the 1800 Home Church Tannenberg organ. Owen recommends restoration of the latter and rerestoration of the former. The following is from Owen's April 1989 report:

> Despite its thoroughly battered appearance, the Home Church organ is remarkably intact and eminently restorable. As the largest extant example of Tannenberg's work as well as the only extant two-manual Tannenberg organ, it is of overwhelming historical and musical importance . . . I think that the circumstance that we all find exciting is that the Home Church organ . . . is nearing its 200th anniversary. This heightens its interest and relevance to historians, musicians, and of course, Moravians and North Carolinians. Probably very few of the latter realize that their state harbors one of the most historic organs in the entire country.

1989   Paula Locklair enters into negotiations with Home Church pastor Robert Sawyer to explore the interest of the church in this project. Sawyer wrote, "The staff and official boards of Home Church have reviewed your recent correspondence concerning the restoration of the Tannenberg organ presently stored in MESDA. We are in agreement that it would be a very fine project and would prove beneficial in many ways . . . Please be assured of our continued interest and support of your proposal for restoration. . . ." June 14, 1989.

1992   February—the Home Church organ is officially loaned to Old Salem Inc. The only obstacle that remains is where to put the organ after restoration.

1998   The organ is assembled by Taylor & Boody Organbuilders as an exhibit in Old Salem's Horton Center Gallery to see for sure how much of the original survived. A decision was made to house the restored organ in an auditorium in the new visitor center for Old Salem, a building that was still in the planning phase.

1999   After the exhibit closed, the organ was moved to the Taylor & Boody shop in Staunton, Virginia.

2002   The bellows for the organ, still in the Home Church attic, are also loaned to Old Salem for restoration by Taylor & Boody.

2003   March—The bellows are removed from the attic and taken to Taylor & Boody for restoration.

2004   February 1–March—The restored organ is installed in the new Old Salem Visitor Center; rededication festivities are held March 19–21; David Tannenberg's 276th birthday is March 21, 2003.

APPENDIX II: THE TAYLOR & BOODY TANNENBERG RESTORATION TEAM

Ryan Albashian: General assembly of the organ

Kelley Blanton, Head Case Maker: Case and console restoration and carving restoration

Chris Bono: New keyboard construction; console parts and general assembly of organ; and initial organ setup in Salem

John Boody: Bellows frame construction; wood procurement; first studies of Salem organ; and initial organ setup in Salem

Larry Damico: Initial organ setup in Salem

Sarah Grove-Humphries: Playing action restoration

Tom Karaffa: Windchest restoration and general assembly of organ

Robbie Lawson, Head Pipe Maker: Restoration of metal pipes; bellows removal from Home Church attic; case paint stripping; and general photo documentation

Christoph Metzler, Pipe Restoration Specialist: Restoration of façade pipes, assisted by Robbie Lawson, and restoration work on metal pipes

Chris Peterson: Bellows restoration and wind system repair

Jeff Peterson: Restoration of metal pipes

Holly Regi: Case and façade pipe paint stripping and repairs

Bruce Shull, Project Manager: Organ documentation; measured CAD drawings; tonal repairs and finishing; initial setup of organ in Salem; bellows removal from Home Church attic, and research work on all extant Tannenberg organs

George Taylor: Research work on extant Tannenberg organs; expertise from 1970 restoration of 1802 Tannenberg organ in Madison, Virginia

Daniel Thomas: Case repair and paint stripping

Emerson Willard: Moving the organ to Staunton and general assembly of the organ

1800 Tannenberg Organ—Home Moravian Church, Salem, North Carolina, Pipe Measurements

Hauptwerk, Metal Pipes		Cutup	Body OD	Wall Thickness Top	Wall Thickness Mouth	Mouth Width	Cutup/ Mouth W	Foot Length
Principal 8'	D	22.9	123.2	1.04	1.52	94.5	0.24	370
	c	16.2	80.2	1.01	1.17	62.4	0.26	380
	c'	9.9	48.4	0.78	1.07	37.2	0.27	355
	c''	5.8	29.2	0.68	0.79	22	0.26	151.7
	c'''	3.6	17.6	0.69	0.72	12.7	0.28	150.6
	f''	3.4	14.1	0.72		10.2	0.33	148.5
Quintadena 8'	C	20.5	83.8	0.94	1.27	63	0.33	201
	c	11.2	50.1	0.88	0.93	38	0.29	171
	c'	6.8	30.8	0.69	0.82	22.7	0.30	150
	c''	4.9	18.4	0.57	0.66	13.4	0.37	146
	c'''	3.0	11.2	0.66		7.6	0.39	146
	ds'''	2.3	10.2	0.55		7	0.33	145.2
Principal Octav 4'	C	13.8	77.5	0.95	1.31	56.6	0.24	224
	c	9.5	48	0.71	0.93	37	0.26	170.8
	c'	6	29.6	0.62	0.82	21.5	0.28	150
	c''	3.9	17.5	0.59		12.2	0.32	147.6
	c'''	2.4	10.6	0.58		7.1	0.34	146.5
	e'''		9.4	0.54				139.5
Quinte 3'	C	11.3	57.2	0.81	1.14	43	0.26	214.5
	c	6.7	34.5	0.67	0.83	25.3	0.26	150.3
	c'	4.3	20.6	0.57	0.66	15.2	0.28	139.7
	c''	3.1	12.7	0.56		8.7	0.36	140
	c'''	1.7	8.4	0.55		5.8	0.29	140
	f'''	1.5	6.9	0.50		4.4	0.34	141.3
Sup Octav 2'	C	9.5	46.1	0.62	0.91	35.1	0.27	186
	c	5.7	28.1	0.57	0.81	20.9	0.27	141
	c'	3.6	16.8	0.62	0.64	12	0.30	139.5
	c''	2.3	10.7	0.49		7	0.33	139.9
	c'''	1.5	7.1	0.45		4.6	0.33	142
	f'''	1.4	6.6	0.55		3.8	0.37	141

(table continues)